HOW TO SPEAK PIRATE

A Treasure Chest of Seafaring Slang

By Geordie Telfer

ARCTIC
RAVEN

The Publisher: Arctic Raven Publishing Ltd.

Library and Archives Canada Cataloguing in Publication

Telfer, Geordie

How to speak pirate : a treasure chest of seafaring slang / Geordie
Telfer.

ISBN-13: 978-0-9694977-8-3
ISBN-10: 0-9694977-8-4

1. Pirates—Terminology. I. Title.

G535.T45 2008   910.4'5   C2007-906009-9

Project Director: Yvonne Harris
Project Editor: Kathy van Denderen
Book Design & Layout: Jodene Draven
Front Cover Image: © Photoshow / Dreamstime.com
Back Cover Image: © Andreas Meyer / Dreamstime.com

PC: P5

Contents

Dedication

To the memory of Robert Newton

(ARR. I. P.)

Acknowledgments

I would like to ~~acknowledge~~ thank ~~my editor~~ Kathy van Denderen, my editor, for preserving (and clarifying) this work with ~~it's~~ its sense of ~~humour~~ humor intact.

How to Use This Book

Ahoy, me hearties! The first half of *How to Speak Pirate* is divided into seven chapters. In the unlikely event that you actually want to carry on a conversation in Lingua Pira, Chapters 1–7 are organized into topics that should help you to find the word or phrase you're looking for. In the more likely event that you simply want to be entertained by outlandish mouthfuls of salty words, you should *still* read Chapters 1–7, because they will get both your tongue and your brain limbered up for the second part of the book: the Lingua Pira Lexicon.

The lexicon is a dictionary of pirate terms that will be immensely useful the next time you're in a room full of *buccaneers* and feel left out. Words in *italics* are cross-references to other terms found in the Lingua Pira Lexicon. Finally, Lingua Pira is meant to be spoken aloud. Do not hesitate to read portions of this book aloud to your friends, lover(s), spouse(s), children, pets or furniture—it will almost certainly suffuse you with the warm glow of high seas thievery. Let the *palaver* begin!

Introduction

What Is Lingua Pira?

Speaking Pirate is not an exact science. After all, it's not a language you can learn by flying off to "Piraq" or "Piranada" or even the "United States of Piratica" (though many would debate this last one). No, speaking Pirate is all about unleashing your inner *rogue* (or *wench*, as the case may be) upon an unsuspecting world. Happily, the building blocks of this so-called language have more to do with fun, creativity and self-expression than with tongue-twisting mouthfuls of *argle-bargle*, *jaw breakers* or *sleeveboards*. In short, Lingua Pira is more a state of mind than a vocabulary of rules.

The term "Lingua Franca" refers to a language that is spoken beyond the boundaries of its native country. It can also mean a language commonly understood between two people but that is neither of their mother tongues. And finally, it can refer to a sort of hybrid language that acts as a bridge between two different cultures. To describe the lingo of the worldwide pirate community, the most apt term is Lingua Pira (pronounced "lin-gwa py-rah"), and hereafter when you see the term "Lingua Pira," this is what it means.

For readers who may be wondering how Lingua Pira can make a positive difference in their lives, just imagine the impression you'll make the first time you burst into a room and say, *"Ahoy, me hearties! Shall we away* to a *groggery* for a *mutchkin* or a *quintal* of *barley oil?*" And whether you're a *rogue* or a *wench*, Lingua Pira can help you to meet that special someone— admittedly, that special someone may be a *buccaneer* of love who will first steal your heart and then bury it on a beach before ultimately losing the treasure map—but what a *special buccaneer* that *buccaneer* will be! How could amorous *freebooters* do anything but respond favorably when told that they're *hugsome* or that they *spread much cloth?*

The other thing to remember is that yesteryear's pirate ship is today's office, and herein you will find many expressions to describe difficult or incompetent personalities, be they at sea, in the adjacent cubicle or both. For instance, next time the surly computer *swab* mutters under his breath about doing his job, just call him a *grumbletonian* and see if he doesn't understand. Did the vapid *maiden* from payroll mess up the checks again? Next time, try calling her a *crumpet-witted bessie lorch* and see if the situation doesn't improve (it probably won't). And finally, if your boss/captain is sensitive about his (or her) hair loss, try using the word *balditude* as a way of demonstrating that you share the discomfiture of your superiors. Promotion is sure to follow!

The main thing to remember is that Lingua Pira should be spoken aloud. Indeed, many people report a rascally glow of good feeling after voicing exclamations such as:

Shiver me timbers!

Futtocks!

Neptune's goblets!

It's going to take a bit of practice, but try to work Lingua Pira into your everyday life. For instance, if upon waking up you see rain pouring down, say aloud "Arr! The day be a *blashy* one." Immediately, you own the day, rather than it owning you. You may also find that many colorful words for everyday items seep into daily life. Something as mundane as getting dressed in the morning becomes an adventure in thrilling possibility. Do you twist yourself into knots every day deciding whether to say "pants" or "trousers"? Well, tie yourself down, because now you've also got *bumbags, galligaskins* and *sit upons* to choose from. Or instead of asking your barista for coffee with two sugars and two creams, you may demand twice the *tooth rot* and double the *butter broth*. And of course, pirate pet owners can take their *tail waggers* for a walk, while the *purring bandits* stay at home.

On good days, Lingua Pira can help each of us to steer our course, since we are, after all, the captains of our own destinies. On bad days, a few words of Lingua Pira can remind us that even when you feel stuck in the *doldrums* of life, at any moment, a sail may appear over the horizon, bringing with it the possibility of adventure, romance, riches and, of course, hope!

Lingua Pira—speak it proudly.

PART ONE

Chapter One

How Did Pirates Speak?

You may have noticed that the title of this book is *How to Speak Pirate,* and not *How Pirates Really Spoke.* There is a good reason for this, and that is because we don't actually know how pirates really spoke. The so-called Golden Age of Piracy lasted from about 1680 to 1730. Audio recording was not invented until 1877 when Thomas Edison was trying to think of a way to record telephone messages. Newspapers were certainly widespread, but the sit-down interview with "quotes" didn't exist yet, and at any rate, pirates were not the sorts to have journalists on board their ships. Having said all that though, we can make some educated guesses about the way pirates might have spoken.

The first thing to remember is that pirates were, first and foremost, sailors. Sailors had their own special lingo for the day-to-day operation of large sailing ships and also developed their own slang for things that had nothing to do with sailing. To modern ears, the eccentric phrases and salty idioms of sailors from long ago would sound more than a little like Lingua Pira. The second thing to remember is that although sailors and pirates spent many weeks or months at sea, they often went ashore, where they would also soak up slang expressions in use by *landlubbers*. With these resources, pirates who wanted to speak only in colorfully outrageous phrases had no trouble coming up with material.

One of the notions that makes the idea of pirates so attractive is that we think of them as rebellious *free-booters* living by no one's rules but their own; indeed, any attempt to speak like them should reflect this quality. The Lingua Pira Lexicon, the second part of this book, is a dictionary of nautical and slang terms that pirates might have used. Although the terms will undoubtedly be useful in helping you to speak Lingua Pira, you should feel free to make up your own expressions—in short, break the rules (of which there really are none anyway). If you're tired of resting your head on a pillow all the time, just pick up a thesaurus and go to sleep on a *noggin bolster*. Bored by doing dishes? Try thinking of yourself as a *trencher-wipe*. Tired of being single? Why not try being *gloriously free* instead?

The Proper Use of "Arr"

If your idea of how to talk like a pirate involves speaking with the rounded R's of "Arr," and in fact starting every sentence with "Arr," then you've got a long way to go. The ridiculous notion that all pirates spoke like this can be traced to the inspired performance of Robert Newton as Long John Silver in the 1954 film adaptation of *Treasure Island*. Newton was from

Dorset, England, and played the part with his natural "West Country" accent. When he pronounces the name Jim Hawkins, it is "Jim H*or*kins," and so his many exclamations of "Arr" are colorful renderings of "Ah," as in "I see" or maybe even "Uh," in situations where he needs a few seconds to formulate a rascally response to some incriminating line of questioning. He was such a success that he went on to play Silver again in the sequel and yet again in a 13-part mini-series. Robert Newton is recognized as having set the gold standard for all subsequent portrayals of pirates and is officially recognized as the "patron saint" of Talk Like a Pirate Day (see Afterword: Celebrating Your Pirate Heritage).

The expression "Arr" appears nowhere in the novel *Treasure Island* by Robert Louis Stevenson, first published in 1881. It appears in no known pirate films prior to Newton's performance in 1954. Neither does it appear in the lexicons of sailor's slang, nor in the dictionaries of regular slang used as references for this book. In spite of this, there will always be people who argue that pirates really spoke like this anyway, and the answer is that if they were from the West Country like Robert Newton and were expressing understanding or stalling for time, then, yes, they *might* have said "Arr." And in all fairness, it must be admitted that the infamous pirate Edward Teach (a.k.a. Blackbeard) is thought to have been from Bristol and might have had such an accent. In addition, Sir Francis Drake (explorer, privateer and later pirate) was from Devon, and so he, too, may have uttered an "Arr" or two in his time.

There are a few other circumstances in which pirates might have actually said "Arr." One theory is that "Arr" is a bastardization of "Aye." Long before it became doubled into the "Aye, aye" of nautical lore, "Aye" was in use by all manner of landlubbers as another word for "yes," and there are certainly any number of West Country dialects that might roll "Aye" into "Arr." Be aware then, that when you say "Arr," you may be assenting to some piratical undertaking. Also worth noting is the archaic expression "arrah," which is defined as "an Anglo-Irish expletive of emotion, excitement." The modern misuse of "Arr" seems to have more in common with "arrah," since it is usually uttered as an all-purpose exclamation without its own meaning. Undeniably, though, "Arr" is incredibly useful to speakers of Lingua Pira because blurting it out gives you a couple of extra seconds to come up with something a bit more piratical to say. It appears frequently in the Lingua Pira Lexicon, but wherever possible, it is used to mean "yes" or "I agree." Utter it judiciously, but with great conviction and gnashing of teeth (if you have some).

In closing, once again, Lingua Pira is all about breaking rules and living (or at least speaking) on your own terms. A few words or phrases of Lingua Pira can fill you with a warm glow of rebellious confidence. It can put combative co-workers in their places. It can give you a feeling of self-reliant empowerment. Or it can simply make for interesting conversation at the next party where you find yourself sitting across from someone with a friendly sparkle in his or her one remaining eye.

Chapter Two

Getting Started

Picking a Pirate Name

If you're going to talk like a pirate, you must be able to introduce yourself effectively. The first thing to do is make yourself a chart and fill it in as you see fit. Here are some guidelines on how to create a chart with three columns:

Left-Hand Column: Insert an Adjective or Noun

Go for something colorful that's going to make an impression. Words, such as *boring, mundane* and *inconsequential,* are NOT recommended for inclusion here. Instead, think of colorful piratey words, such as *daggerknee, groggified, hugsome* or *bumsquabbled.*

Center Column: Insert a Given Name

Pick a name that is either masculine or feminine. Given that anybody has half a chance getting this right, you'd be surprised at how many pirates pick inappropriate names from either gender, such as Harpo, Alannis, Adolf or Oprah.

Right-Hand Column: Insert an Additional Descriptor (optional)

If you've struck out in the left hand column, now's the time to make up for it by adding a lurid descriptor of either sanguinary rage, jolly opulence or carnal appeal.

Choose Ye Name Hereunder

Adjective or Noun	Given Name	Additional Descriptor (optional)
Black	Ned	(the) Bloodthirsty
Gunpowder	Bart	(the) Fancy
Scurvy	Joe	(the) Forgetful
Big	Mary	(the) Angry
Cannonball	Kate	(the) Beautiful
Gassy	Polly	(the) Ugly
Barnacle	Suzie	(the) Strong
Diamond	Bob	(the) One-Eyed
Swordfish	Ignatius	(the) Flatulent

Now, mix and match either or both of the outer columns with the middle one until you get something you like, but a word of caution: the wrong combination will make you sound like either a washed-up folk singer (Big One-Eyed Mary) or a second-rate prize fighter (Beautiful Joe Diamond). Names like this should be avoided at all costs.

To start with, you may want to stick to combinations from the first and second columns *only*: Scurvy Suzie, Bloodthirsty Bart, Cannonball Polly, Swordfish Kate, Gassy Ignatius and so on.

Commonly Used Words and Phrases

The main thing to remember is that to *speak* Pirate, you have to *feel* like a pirate, and to *feel* like a pirate, it helps to *speak* Pirate. It's a vicious circle, but a fun one, involving lots of merriment and people dressed in funny outfits. Begin by finding someone else who wants to learn Pirate, and spend long hours *carousing* with them—you won't learn anything, but you'll have a lot of fun and may inadvertently start a family.

The key thing to remember is: Practice! Practice! Practice! Maybe your community has a Pirates Benevolent Society (maybe, but probably not). Or perhaps the local Legion sponsors weekly *Buccaneer* Mixers (again, the odds of this are slim). And finally, you may be able to find other aspiring speakers of Lingua Pira by trying Pirate Speed Dating in which 25 hopefuls meet 25 pirates in 25 minutes (however, this notion is completely fictional, so don't get your hopes up).

At any rate, the best way to begin is not so much by *speaking* as *thinking* in Lingua Pira. To that end, you will find below, handy charts that provide piratical translations of many useful and common phrases.

Greeting Friends

Lubber Speak	Lingua Pira
Hello friends!	*Ahoy, mateys!*
The weather this morning is excellent, my good colleagues!	'Tis a *proud mornin' me hearties!*
I beg your pardon?	*Anan?*
Whose step is that I hear behind me?	Was that yer *beetle-crushing tread, dimsel wit?*

Addressing Friends Who Have Wooden Legs

There are many affectionate forms of address for friends with *wooden legs* that have more merit than the overused "Peg Leg." You should feel free to make up your own in keeping with the specific friend you are addressing, but here are some starters:

- *Plank Shank*
- *Lumber Limb*
- *Splinter Toe*
- *Spruce Boot*
- *Pine Foot*

Describing the Weather

As you can see, *proud mornin'* describes favorable weather conditions, but there are far more interesting expressions for bad or inclement weather.

Lubber Speak	Lingua Pira
It is raining cats and dogs, and there is a strong gale.	'Tis *blowin' great guns and small arms.*
Be cautious, for the day is a rainy one and the footing is slippery.	Step careful fer the day be a *blashy* one, and the decks are *clarty.*
I say, those waves have appeared on the surface of the water for no good reason.	There be *bottom wind.*
The wind is very aggressive, and there are many sudden squalls of rain.	'Tis a *right blustrous* day with a lot o' *blunk* flyin' about.
Those ominous clouds appear to presage a heavy downpour.	Them *storm breeders* are just waitin' to pelt us with *Scotch mist.*

Going to the Store

If you insist on speaking Lingua Pira at your local convenience or grocery store, you almost certainly won't get what you want, but you will have positively affected someone else's day, by causing them extreme puzzlement. You will notice that some of the expressions are simply creative turns of phrase that do not even appear in the Lingua Pira Lexicon.

Lubber Speak	Lingua Pira
I would like a dozen of your finest eggs.	I'll take a *kintle* o' yer choicest *chicken jewels*.
I would like 12 bottles of beer.	A *kintle* o' yer finest *brownstone, matey*.
Have you any cigarettes, my surly clerk?	Got any *nose warmers*, ye *trout-faced swab*?
I should like a large cup of tea.	I'll be needin' to *get* meself *around* a *mutchkin* o' *scandal broth*.
Coffee. Double-double. Large, please.	Sling me a *jorum* of java, me *hearty*. Twice the *tooth rot* and double the *butter broth*.
I would like a coffee with sugar and no cream.	Make me java sweet as love and dark as the night.
I would like a black coffee.	Brew mine pure 'n' shimmerin' like obsidian.

Visiting the Doctor

If you're going to see your doctor, we don't recommend describing your affliction in the terms outlined below, but you can try if you want.

Lubber Speak	Lingua Pira
My left foot has recently begun to emit a foul odor.	Me *portside hind shifter's* come over all *gamey* lately.
My feet are aching.	Me *hind shifters* are sore.
My head aches constantly due to incipient alcoholism.	Me *noggin*'s forever poundin' on account o' me bein' such an incorrigible *spigot sucker*.
My bottom is feeling ticklish.	There be itches in me *britches*. Me *double juggs* are feelin' crawly. Me *Sunday face* is wearin' a smirk. Me *monocular eyeglass* has got some grit in it.
My stomach is upset.	Me *belly* feels like there's a *broadside* underway.

Lubber Speak	Lingua Pira
I am troubled by chronic flatulence.	Me *bottom wind* knows no limits. Lately, the occasional burst o' *pocket thunder* has turned into a *right* storm. I've got *arse music* that just won't stop playin'.
I am troubled by a non-specific feeling of general malaise.	I'm feelin' *right no-howish all-overish* these days.

Parting Advice

Feel free to use the previous examples as a springboard to create your very own Lingua Pira vocabulary. Try to think of creative ways to describe mundane situations in the pirate spirit. Again, don't be concerned with sticking to a particular set of phrases, but revel in making up your own expressions as you move closer to celebrating your inner pirate.

Chapter Three

Drinking

Fermented Bliss

Pirates enjoy their drink. And often, the kind of people who want to talk like pirates themselves enjoy a little *anti-abstinence* now and again—and again and again and again. The famous pirate captain Bartholomew (Black Bart) Roberts was a teetotalling tea-swigger, but he was the exception rather than the rule. He was cursed by a crew whose *back teeth* were always *well afloat,* and at times it was all Black Bart could do to get any work out of them. Drink, drinking and being drunk weren't just the pastimes of choice among sailors and pirates, either. Ashore, as well as at sea, the eager enjoyment of alcohol was as prevalent as its abuse. It isn't surprising then that there is such a wealth of vivid slang to describe fermented beverages, the drinking of same, the effects of same and the eventual regurgitation of same.

Different Ways of Saying You'd Like to Go for a Drink

You and your pirate mates want to get yourselves *irrigated,* but how to make your intentions known? You have to do it with *scurvy* wit and *tough-knuckled* style.

Lubber Speak	Lingua Pira
Shall we go for a quick drink?	Shall we *away* for a *modest quencher?*
Let's have a drink.	Let's *suck up some corn juice.*
Shall we walk to the pub?	Care for a *leg stretcher?*
Do you want a drink?	Try a little *anti-abstinence?*

Asking for Directions to the Nearest Bar

Once you've decided to go for a drink, the next step is to figure out where to go. In all likelihood, it will only be after several expeditions in the field that these words will come trippingly off your tongue in everyday conversation.

Lubber Speak	Lingua Pira
Can you point me to the nearest public house?	What way to make tracks for the nearest *groggery*?
Is there a drinking establishment nearby?	Where be the closest *gargle factory, matey*?
I should like to know the location of a seedy bar where I might become inebriated.	How do I steer a course for a *wobble shop* in these parts?
Where might I savor the bacchanalian delights of wine, women and song?	Have ye got a place of *libation* around here?

What to Drink

Once you've picked a place to imbibe, the next step is deciding what to order. Lingua Pira has many synonyms for beer and whiskey, but happily, none for wine coolers. Not to be discouraging, but if you're planning to order a wine cooler, you are not pirate material.

Beer: *barley oil, belch, belly vengeance, brownstone, bumclink, cold blood, English burgundy, gatter, heavy-wet, knock-me-down, nectar of barley, swizzle*

Whiskey: *barley bree, breaky leg, bottled earthquake, caper juice, curse of Scotland, family disturbance, forty-rod lightning, heel tap, hell broth, liquid fire, mountain dew, neck oil, old man's milk, pine top, rot gut, scumgullion*

Rum and Water: *grog* (a term that also refers to alcoholic beverages in general)

Sangria: *sangaree*

How Much to Order and How Drunk It Will Get You

Pirates would have been drinking rum, and the degrees of drunkenness computed in the right column indicate a volume vs. inebriation ratio that reflects this. However, because many modern speakers of Lingua Pira will prefer to substitute beer for spirits, they will have to make those calculations themselves.

Pirate Measure	Approximation of Present-Day Volume Equivalency	Pirate Rating of Drunkenness
dram, gum tickler, toothful	less than an ounce	*muggy:* tipsy (or warm)
modest quencher, noggin	about one-quarter pint	*groggified:* pleasantly drunk

Pirate Measure	Approximation of Present-Day Volume Equivalency	Pirate Rating of Drunkenness
mutchkin	a pint	*back teeth well afloat:* good and drunk
keg	indeterminate (a lot)	*both sheets aft:* very drunk
quintal	weighing at least 100 lbs	alcohol poisoning imminent

The Act of Drinking

Once you've got a drink in your belly, you may start thinking up creative ways to describe what you're doing. Here are a few to get you started.

- *bleeding the monkey*
- *carousing*
- getting *irrigated*
- partaking of *libation*
- *quaffing*
- *splicing the main brace*
- *sucking up some corn juice*

Describing Other Drinkers

A word to the wise: Use the following list discreetly when describing people you don't really know, because there is no way to predict the effects of speaking Lingua Pira to complete strangers.

- *ale knight*
- *elbow crooker*
- *spigot sucker*
- *lushington*

The Effects of Drink

Once you've had a few, certain unmistakable changes in appearance or behavior will begin to manifest themselves. These are described below, with their appropriate translation into Lingua Pira.

Lubber Speak	Lingua Pira
red nosed	*malmsey nosed*
face-flushed red	sportin' a *grog blossom*
unsteady on your feet	*quade*
falling-over drunk	*listing groundward*

Lubber Speak	Lingua Pira
throwing up	*casting accounts*
	hurling yer hardtack
	lobbing the keg
	spewing the oakum

Responsible *Carousing*

Of course, we cannot stress strongly enough the importance of *carousing* responsibly. The popular pirate bumper sticker that says, "Don't drink and sail; ye might spill yer *rum*," makes light of an all too serious problem. And remember that even though a bit of tonsil lubrication can loosen your inhibitions when making the acquaintance of *hugsome wenches* and *rogues,* nothing spoils the good times faster than losing your *rum* ration all over their shoes.

At first you may feel that sucking back a few makes you better at speaking Lingua Pira, and up to a point this is probably true. But after one *mutchkin* too many, the old tongue starts to slip, and before you know it, you've just said, "Tiver She Mimbers!" and at that point the game is pretty much over. By all means use *carousing* as an opportunity to practice Lingua Pira, but make sure you know the difference between a *toothful* and a *mutchkin,* between feeling *muggy* and having your *back teeth well afloat.*

Cheers!

Chapter Four

Ordering in Restaurants

Pirates didn't necessarily spend a lot of time in restaurants, because they were usually at sea. However, when shore leave came along after a profitable bit of *plundering,* the first thing the crew would do was go ashore and spend all their treasure shares on wine and *wenches.* After weeks or months of barely digestible shipboard rations, most of them probably gorged themselves on all the fancy food they could get. But some of them must have grown accustomed to the vile fare they were fed at sea and might have preferred *burgoo, loblolly* and *conjee* to the fancier dishes they could find *dryside.*

Aspiring speakers of Lingua Pira would do well to remember that pirate manners are not generally socially acceptable in today's environment of gender and socio-economic neutrality. Similarly, most of the food items that pirates might have ordered are entirely unknown to purveyors of haute cuisine. But for those of you whose membership in the Society for Creative Anachronism has not lapsed, a smorgasbord of pirate delicacies can be found under "What to Order."

Expressing Hunger

Simply saying, "I'm hungry," doesn't cut it. Other speakers of Lingua Pira will look down on you and may in fact revoke your honorary *wooden leg*. Again, try to be creative. The phrases outlined below will get you started, but don't be afraid to go beyond or even overboard; try to think of nautical similes for hunger: "*Me belly* be a veritable maelstrom of emptiness," "*Me* innards are rumblin' like a *grampus*," or even "The sails of me stomach are stuck in the *doldrums* of starvation" (though you won't win any awards for that one). Anyway, start with these:

- "Me guts have got no nourishment."
- "Arr, *matey*, the *stomach worm gnaws*."
- "I'm *savage as a meat axe*."
- "I've been *dinin' with Duke Humphrey*."
  (This expression often refers to going hungry for an extended period of time; for instance, if you're flat broke.)

And here are a couple of phrases that express a desire to actually eat, as opposed to just a state of being hungry.

- "I'd like to *get* meself *around* some *victuals*."
- "Time to *choke the luff*."

What to Order

Once you've found yourself a *grub dive,* it's time to choose some *victuals.* If you're looking for trouble, ordering a meal in Lingua Pira is a good way to start. About the only useful phrase for modern diners might be: "I'd like some *flesh* and *grass,*" meaning, "meat and vegetables." If you're feeling particularly fightsome, try substituting *bunny grub* for "vegetables." Now and again, you will find an establishment that actually serves a version of the perennial pirate favorite, *salmagundi,* but beyond that, just try walking into an eatery and ordering any of the following:

- *burgoo*
- *calaloo*
- *conjee*
- *loblolly*
- *lobscouse*
- *flummery*
- *hardtack*

And for dessert, try asking for *midshipman's nuts.*

Interacting with Wait Staff

By placing an order for any of the above items, you've pretty much drawn a line in the sand, and whatever the server throws back, you richly deserve. At any rate, a few more cautionary words here are appropriate. Before you can order, you need to get the attention of your server. In this day and age, wait staff in restaurants have as many good reasons to want to slit someone's throat as did the lowliest tavern wretch in the Golden Age of Piracy. Bear this in mind as you read on.

If your server is female, bellowing, *"Ahoy, saucy wench"* is only advisable if you're attending some sort of fancy-dress festival where this sort of thing is expected. Under no circumstances is this form of address advised in the real world (see previous comment on throat slitting). Conversely, if your server is a male, and you are a female, he may in fact enjoy being hailed thusly, *"Ahoy, hugsome rogue."* However, if you are male and choose to hail another male server as so indicated, again, make sure the circumstances are appropriate.

Table Manners

This section will be necessarily brief. About the only use pirates had for cutlery was detaching other pirates from their limbs. Hands (if still attached) were probably the eating utensils of choice. However, for anyone delusional enough to imagine that there might be some sort of pirate table etiquette, we offer the following gem of Lingua Pira: "Quit eatin' with yer hands and use yer *gobstick.*"

Delivering a Verdict on Your Meal

Once you've *et* your meal, a variety of responses may be appropriate. Keep in mind that chefs and kitchen staff have ready access to sharp instruments capable of inflicting gruesome carnage. Frankly, they have more pirate armament than you do.

Lubber Speak	Lingua Pira
That food was most tasty.	Them *victuals* was *right throatsome*.
Our meal was exceptional.	Them eats was a real *snorter*.
Those comestibles were outstanding.	That *grub* was *ripper*.
It was worse than sewage.	I've had *bilge* water that tasted better.
It was comparable to hempen fibers impregnated with tar.	It tasted like *oakum*.
It had the taste and consistency of rotten tobacco.	'Twas like a dish o' *mundungus*.

Getting Thrown Out of Restaurants

If you've followed the meal-ordering formula as outlined, ejection from the premises is almost certain to crop up on the menu—most likely towards the end. Remember, pirates have been getting thrown out of taverns and inns since time immemorial, and if this happens to you, you can feel proud. Once you've been vanquished, your day is pretty much over, and you should stand down—after all, you asked for it. Remember, too, that no self-respecting pirate is going to turn around and say, "You'll be hearing from my lawyer!" because pirates, by their very natures, operate outside the law. If you haven't paid your bill (and really, if you're being thrown out, you probably haven't yet), the simplest and most dignified response is to stand tall and say:

"He who eats and runs away, lives to eat another day."

or

"If ye *get* yerself *around victuals* and then turn tail and flee, ye'll be able to *get* yerself *around victuals* and turn and flee some other time."

Chapter Five

Meeting Pirates of the Opposite (or any) Sex

Being a pirate is sexy. Talking like a pirate is sexy, too. Of course, it all depends on the pirate doing the being and the talking, but few would argue that having a ready store of *ribald* talk on the tip of your tongue certainly increases the odds of finding treasure when you dig. This chapter covers the ups and downs of pirate love, from expressing admiration for the pirate whose spot you'd like to mark with an "*X*," to describing the duds who wouldn't stand a chance if they were the last *freebooters* on the seven seas. As always, speak these words with caution and restraint, because you never know whether you'll be the cannonball or the target.

Favorable Terms of Admiration

Whew! Where to begin. Say what you will, sailors and pirates are an imaginative lot with no shortage of colorful expressions to describe someone carnally attractive. Most of the terms are unisex, but a few can be applied only to men or only to women.

hugsome: Can be used to describe either *rogues* or *wenches* and has the advantage of sounding cuddly and non-threatening when it really means you'd like to jump their *crossbones* and *jolly roger* them until the break of day (or the breaking of the bed, whichever comes first).

spreads much cloth: Refer to the Lingua Pira Lexicon in the second half of this book for more details, but simply put, this phrase means that the luster believes that the lustee fills his or her clothes in a most excellent fashion.

fetching: Usually used to describe a well-turned-out *wench* but occasionally used to describe *rogues* as well. The suggestion seems to be that the pirate in question looks so appealing that you'd go fetch him or her wherever that person may be. This phrase is not exclusive to pirates or sailors but has a pleasingly archaic ring to it.

jolly: Nowadays this describes pirates who bowl people over with the breadth of their joyous personalities, but back in the Golden Age of Piracy, it might also describe pirates who had many admirers, thanks in part to the girth of their generous waistlines.

bouncer: This word's literal meaning is a gun or cannon that kicks violently when fired. Applied to an attractive pirate, it means that you think the person would be a lively bunkmate (that is, one who kicks violently when fired).

nice *aft*: A term used to describe the rear of a ship (*aft*), or to describe the rear of a person.

***long-necked goose*:** This can describe a handsome man or a well-endowed one. (See the Lingua Pira Lexicon for more details.)

***ram rod*:** An obviously suggestive epithet derived from the action of the rod used to vigorously pack shot and powder into cannon barrels.

***fair*:** This particular compliment can cause quite a bit of confusion in the present day because it means more or less "average" or "medium." But knights errant, mustachioed villains and, of course, pirates, know that it really means "angelically beautiful."

Describing the Duds

There are some suitors that no self-respecting pirate would touch with a 10-foot barge pole. Sadly, though, it is often only *after* self-respecting pirates *have* touched these suitors (in fact, all over and with any-thing but a barge pole) that this enlightening self-knowledge arrives. Here now are a few choice phrases to describe the ones we all ought to steer clear of.

dead cargo: It's a story familiar to us all—a pirate chum describes his or her new *paramour* in glowing terms, but when you meet said *paramour,* the person turns out to be either a vapid *maiden* or a sniveling *milquetoast.* When high hopes are dashed, we call the object of those hopes *dead cargo.*

fumble fisted: When the moment of passion arrives, how does your pirate *paramour* acquit himself (or herself)? Does she *heave handsomely* or yank your chain? Does he gently *unfurl* your sail or is another yard of good canvas ruined? These clumsy but well-intentioned bunkmates are termed *fumble fisted.*

channel groper: This term actually describes ships that would skulk about in the English Channel, protecting British interests from pirates, smugglers and enemy vessels. Nowadays, though, it describes any unwelcome advance from someone too free with his or her hands. To assume that it's only men who fall into this category would be a mistake; this writer can attest to the existence of more than a few female *channel gropers* (they're never the ones you *want* to grope your channel, either).

half widowed: A woman married to a lazy, shiftless man. To be fair, we've all seen cases of the opposite as well, but "half widowered" just sounds dumb, and so the male of the species suffers in silence.

What Type of Pirate Are You?

If you're male, here are your possibilities:

milquetoast: There really aren't a lot of *milquetoast* pirates. The mere state of "milquetoastery" generally precludes you from even setting foot on a ship, but hey, it takes all kinds, right? *Milquetoasts* are usually the submissive individuals in any relationship, be it personal, professional or piratical. They're happy enough to pick up a shovel and dig but too timid to actually claim their fair share of treasure. They are not team players and suffer from a severe deficit of any sort of life force whatsoever.

rogue: This type of pirate happily engages in *devilry* when the mood strikes him or the opportunity presents itself, but he is not necessarily an all-out *bangster*. *Rogues* have something to say in any given situation (unlike *milquetoasts*) and have enjoyably irreverent personalities (also unlike *milquetoasts*). They are good at being part of a crew or working alone.

bangster: This is a wild, lawless sort who follows only his own path. It's tempting to think that all pirates are *bangsters,* but a lot of them are *rogues* (and of course the occasional *milquetoast*). *Bangsters* are good at leading (often just because they're more insane than anyone else). They may be self-reliant, but they are not good team players.

If you're female, here are your options:

maiden: This is a woman who tends to be rather vapid and helpless, uninterested in anything except, perhaps, what others are interested in. As with *milquetoasts, maidens* suffer from a complete lack of personality or capacity for creative thought. In modern-day terms, *maidens* are well represented in the legions of people who have only started doing yoga because it could be accessorized by carrying little mats around.

wench: All the *rogues* want to meet *wenches,* and with good reason. *Wenches* are strong, self-reliant and totally fun, many having unambiguously friendly sparkles in their eyes. If *maidens* blow over in the slightest of breezes, *wenches* will stand tall in the fiercest of *hurleblasts;* in short, *wenches* are the "total package."

virago: A woman with a strong, forceful personality that makes her not only likely to become a pirate but also to attract other pirates. That being said, like *bangsters, viragos* aren't exactly easy to get along with, and attempts to cuddle up to them at night may be met by forceful expulsion. *Viragos* also make good leaders but are not team players.

What Kind of Pirate Are You Compatible With?

No one wants to fess to being a *milquetoast* or
a *maiden* (again the presence of a little rolled-up yoga
mat in the corner may suggest that you follow the
herd), but that really doesn't matter, because the only
two types of pirates who are really incompatible are
bangsters and *viragos.* A relationship between these
two is like a ship full of gunpowder just waiting to
explode.

rogues and *wenches:* This pairing will make both
parties happy, and a roughly equal relationship will
follow (even if one or the other has a yoga mat rolled
up in the corner).

milquetoasts and *maidens:* A union of perfect banal-
ity, worthy of no more ink.

bangsters and *wenches,* or *bangsters* and *maidens:*
The union may not be a happy one, but it will probably be stable, even more so if a *maiden* is involved,
because, in all likelihood, she lacks the self-awareness
to realize that she is merely a satellite to the central
personality of the *bangster.* A *wench* will have a harder
time enduring a relationship with a *bangster* because
of her greater force of personality, but she will mostly
likely brave it out.

viragos and *rogues,* or *viragos* and *milquetoasts:*
Again, the *milquetoast* will not be aware of any other possibilities in life, while the *virago* will be so concerned with her own self-actualization that the *milquetoast* will barely constitute an irrelevancy on the horizon. *Rogues,* obviously, are unlikely to respond well to this sort of treatment, but a good many will stick it out with a *virago,* while other *rogues* will simply go off and find themselves a suitable *wench.*

The Act Itself

There are plenty of ways to describe the act of pirate love, and none of them are delicate. For instance, if you're feeling bold, ask the *picaroon* of your affections if he or she is up for a bit of old *fore and aft.* Alternately, you might sidle up and simply say, "I'd really like to jump your *crossbones.*"

Assuming that some kind of confrontation has not occurred by this point, you may find yourself lucky enough to wind up in a pirate boudoir (a.k.a the *foc'sle*). This is when you should turn your thoughts to *firkytoodle,* unless of course you are *fumble fisted,* in which case proceeding to the main event may be advisable. At any rate, whether pertaining to the act of undress, or that of "ingress," you should be familiar with the term *heave handsomely,* as this will be useful in any number of circumstances, not all of which involve sex.

Verbs to describe what follows are plentiful, but two of the most piratical are "to *swive*" and "to *jolly roger.*" However, it is highly unlikely that when the moment arrives you will have the presence of mind to use either of these verbs, though your bunkmate will almost certainly be impressed if you do. (If, however, at this juncture it's your mastery of Lingua Pira that both of you are talking about, then there are probably larger issues.)

Preoccupations in the World of Pirate Dating

Pirates are concerned with all the same things that the rest of us are. You may be a woman ready to commit to being a pirate's *paramour,* but as far as he's concerned, you're just his *ligby.* Or you're a male set to ask a woman to be your *first mate,* but she lets on that you're just her *between-the-sheets chum.* And if you are lucky enough to be *bent on a splice* with your pirate *paramour,* then the doubts begin: Is she just after me because my treasure chest is a full one? Does he just like me because my treasure chest is a full one?

Affectionate Forms of Address

All doubts aside, there is no shortage of affectionate names to shower your pirate sweetheart with. A good general rule is to simply stick the word *briny* in front of whatever term of endearment you choose: *ahoy* me *briny* blossom; *ahoy* me *briny buccaneer* and so on. Another nice gesture is to go back to the earlier heading, "Favorable Terms of Admiration," and start lobbing these in whatever combination seems appropriate: *ahoy* me *hugsome wench; avast* ye *jolly rogue*; and so forth. Then just mix and match as necessary: "Ye may be a *milquetoast,* but ye're a *long-necked goose,* too." or "Sure, ye're a vapid *maiden,* but ye *spread much cloth* and I fancy ye for it. Now unfurl yer yoga mat and let's git busy!"

Final Thoughts

In closing, remember that just speaking Lingua Pira gives you an immediate advantage; the object of your affections may not know what a *ligby* is, but he or she will almost certainly want to find out. Certainly, interjecting a few choice phrases of flirtsome pirate speak into the conversation will make for a memorable first date, but it may also turn out to be your last date if you don't pick your subject carefully. However, this is a good way of sorting the *rogues* from the *milquetoasts* and separating the *wenches* from the *maidens.* And now gentle reader, we have given you all the essential tools, and it is time to *dowse the glim* and set sail for pleasure.

Chapter Six

Positive Sentiments and Friendship

There is no doubt that pirates are expert hurlers of insults and seasoned purveyors of salty opinions. But they also try to put a humorous spin on even the direst of situations and eagerly celebrate those rare days when everything goes their way. Furthermore, they make no secret of the value they place on friendship and loyalty. This chapter will introduce you to Lingua Pira's small but select vocabulary to describe good times, exuberant moods and stouthearted friendship.

Agreement

Of course, the simplest way to express agreement in Lingua Pira is to say "Aye." However, if you're feeling a little more creative, you could say, "*I'm thar,*" the pirate equivalent of the surfer's, "I'm there, dude!" Or for those occasions when you meet a new person with whom you see eye patch to eye patch as it were, you can say:

"I like the *cut of yer jib.*"

"I like the *rig of yer sail.*"

or

"You and I *sail on the same boat.*"

Luck and Prosperity

Instead of praising the odds by using the rather lame word "lucky," pirates always describe someone favored by fortune as *arse upwards* or *having the kick.* People who are prosperous can be described as *before the wind,* rolling in *swag*, shod in *booty* or having *plate* falling out of their pockets.

Anything Excellent

Praiseworthy things in piratedom can be described variously as *right, proper* or *thunderin'*; though all of these words can also be used simply for emphasis and flavor. Used more exclusively for things that are good is the term *weatherly,* originally coined to describe a vessel that was "shipshape"; that is, everything in its place and ready for any sort of storm the elements might throw at it. A number of other generic nouns can also be used in place of an excellent object's proper name. Whereas people today might say, "It's a gem," pirates are more likely to say, "It's a *ripper,*" "It's a *snorter,*" or even "That's a *right roarin' meg.*" (For more details on these expressions, see the Lingua Pira Lexicon.) In a somewhat more specific category is the word *quiff,* which refers to an excellent outcome but one achieved by unorthodox means. For example, shutting up a blabbermouth by sticking a parrot down his *grub trap* could be rightly termed a *quiff*.

The Right Sort of People

A *bangster* lives by no one else's rules, and in the pirating world, this is a good thing. To say, "Me friend Wild Susan is a real *bangster*," would generally have all the pirates round the table sitting up and wanting to meet Wild Susan. Opposite, but no less desirable, is the term *suresby,* used to describe someone who is reliable. Although you might think that pirates are simply out to have a good time and hang with *bangsters,* they equally value people they can count on. After all, running a ship is not something you can do alone, and neither is mounting a raiding mission on the governor's warehouse. Finally, if you are an exceptionally able or successful pirate, you might be termed a *haberdasher of grabbery,* suggesting that not only are you good at thieving, but you also do it with dash and style.

Excellent Moods

Good-hearted, jovial pirates may be termed *jolly,* and indeed, bashes and blowouts hosted by these same pirates are often also called *jolly* (though the morning after is rarely described the same way). Although very few pirates can be called sprightly (those who can are perhaps better suited to being leprechauns), a few will bounce out of their bunks in the morning, full of piss and vinegar, and ready to take on the world. This rare breed is often heard to say, "Arr, I'm feelin' *cock-a-hoop* today." And these same pirates are sometimes found wearing their *Friday face,* a smile of relaxed bliss.

Exhorting Others to Positive Action and Bestowing Hearty Affection

It is known that threats of *keelhauling* and hanging-from-the-yard-arm-for-target-practice definitely get results, but many pirate taskmasters realize that you will get more with honey than with vinegar. To that end, sailor lingo in general is full of terms to put a positive spin on getting others to do hard work. When you want a crew of lackadaisical layabouts to sit up and take notice, you can holler, "*Look lively,* mates!" Or when setting some chore that requires verve and snap, you can yell out, "Set about *cheerly!*" or "*Give way with a will!*" Finally, when soliciting opinions on what sort of adventure your crew wants to have (also handy if you have little pirates at home), you can ask, "What feats of *derring-do* shall we do today?" or "What sort of *devilry* shall we get up to today?"

Friendship

Pirates may be quick to call their enemies *scurvy* dogs, *gamey* vermin, *spoliated pilchards,* among other terms, but they also reserve any number of jocose and *tough-knuckled* terms of endearment for those they consider to be their mates. Like many friendships today, this veil of good-natured hostility was a common feature of piratedom. As with all friendly insults, your tone of voice is key; in fact, you could just as easily skip to the next chapter and re-purpose any of the real insults found therein, but with an amiable lilt to your voice. To get you going, here are a few favorites:

- me ancient *fungus*
- me *hearty*
- me *merry Greek*
- me ravenous *messmate*

And that, as they say, is that. If pirates are sparing but creative in the expressions they use to describe good things, they are positively lavish in the diligence and brain power they apply to exclamations, insults and swearing—but that is another chapter.

Chapter Seven

Exclamations, Insults and Swearing

If you've skipped to this chapter first, then you are clearly one of those people who want to know how to swear in as many languages as possible. In pirating terms, this suggests that you might in fact be more concerned with calling your hapless victims *sleeveless lick spittles* than with actually stealing their treasure. At any rate, you are in good company, because for better or for worse, the popular image of pirates today includes the idea that they have salty insults ready to go at a moment's notice. And not just crusty put-downs, but quaintly worded ones with a pleasingly archaic nautical ring.

As already pointed out, in many ways the interpersonal dynamics of the crew on a sailing ship seem to be roughly analogous to those of the modern office or other workplace. Accordingly (and happily) then, there are insults for just about everyone: those who may not be the brightest; those who are lazy; those who are bad-tempered; those who talk too much; those who are incompetent; those who are overbearing; and those whose lips have to pried from the captain's *monocular eyeglass*. In short, no one is left behind.

Prepare then to learn 57 different ways of bestowing a *sailor's blessing*.

Exclamations of Surprise or Alarm

Lubber Speak	Lingua Pira
Well, I'll be!	*Blow me down!*
Good heavens!	*Shiver me timbers!*
Great Caesar's ghost!	*Neptune's goblets!*
Goodness gracious me!	*Gadzooks!*
Ye gods!	*Egads!*

Intelligence (or lack thereof)

Lubber Speak	Lingua Pira
You are an immensely thickheaded person.	Ye're as *thick as the mizenmast.*
You have the cranial capacity of a sparrow.	Thou'rt *right bird-witted.*
Your skull is filled with a broth-like mixture.	*Ahoy, chowder head.*

Lubber Speak	Lingua Pira
Your intelligence is comparable to that of a buttery snack.	Ye're *crumpet witted*.
His eyes lack the bright spark of intelligence.	He's a *proper dabberlack*.
The texture of her brain is surely that of spongy, rotten wood.	She's got *daddick* on the *brain pan*.
Overall, your wits are quick as stagnant water.	Ye're a *dimsel, matey*.
You are a dullard.	Ye're a *dullard*.
Your lack of culture is matched only by your excess of stupidity.	Ye're a *gawpus*.
You are a stupid but good-natured fellow.	Ye're a *gowk*.
You are so lacking in mental acuity that if you were a fish, I could catch you barehanded.	Ye *gumpus!*
Her process of so-called logic is so tortuous that it reminds me of a round turn with two half hitches.	She's *knot-brained*.
You are an ungainly and awkward fellow.	Ye *lubber!*

Sanity and Its Presumed Absence

We all know people who seem just a little (or a lot) "off," and seemingly so are many sailors and pirates.

Lubber Speak	Lingua Pira
Unsound in the head	*Barmy in the crumpet*
A sandwich or two short of a picnic	*Seven pieces short of eight*
Permanently deranged	*Run aground in addle cove*

Laziness, Clumsiness and Incompetence

Lubber Speak	Lingua Pira
You are a lazy fellow.	Ye *belly gut*.
He is a shiftless individual.	He's a *shack rag*.
Collectively, you are an ungainly crew.	Well, if it ain't the *gawky squad*.
This group is gangly and uncoordinated.	What an *awkward squad!*
You are a silly, ineffectual person.	Ye're a *gossoon*.
Your enthusiasm is unsupported by competence.	What a *galoot!*

Lubber Speak	Lingua Pira
Your preparations are not equal to the task.	What sort o' *ragged-arsed* plan is this?
Your alleged reasons for failing are wholly unsupported by the evidence.	That's a *sleeveless* excuse!

Bad Attitudes, Overbearing Demeanors and Ass Kissers

Lubber Speak	Lingua Pira
Stop muttering negatively under your breath.	Quit bein' such a *grumbletonian.*
Hey, sourpuss!	Hoy, *trout face.*
You are an offensive person.	Ye're a *proper rudesby.*
She is the very embodiment of fire and brimstone.	She's *Hades in human form.*
His personality is comparable to a shipboard version of eternal damnation.	He's *hell afloat.*
Her arguments are unsound, her manner is overbearing, and her voice is loud.	She's a real *jaw me down.*

Lubber Speak	Lingua Pira
Obsequious flattery of your superiors will get you nowhere.	Bein' a *lick spittle* will do ye no good.
Do you think that detaching your lips from the boss' posterior is in anyway a possibility?	Stop bein' a *toady*.

Excessive Talkativeness, Boasting and Talking Stupidly

Lubber Speak	Lingua Pira
Your actions do not lend credence to your words.	Ye're *all jaw, like a sheep's head*.
Cease speaking this endless stream of errant nonsense.	Quit yer *circumbendibus*.
Your boasting is becoming tiresome.	Yer *bloviatin's* givin' me an earache.
Your excessive verbalization reminds of a windy day.	Yer manner of speech be *right blustrous*.
She talks a lot.	She's *forty jawed*.
Your confused manner of speaking communicates no meaning to me.	What a load of *argle-bargle*.

Lubber Speak	Lingua Pira
He is in an unfortunate state of perma-speak.	He's *run aground in gabby cove.*
Stop your endless tongue wagging.	Put an end to the *palaver!*

Describing Silliness

Although all of following terms mean different things, using any of them in conversation will successfully convey an impression of ineffectual frivolity relating to the person being described.

- *bandicoot*
- *bessie lorch*
- *gaby*
- *gandflook*
- *gudgeon*

Cheating the Devil

If for some reason you want to avoid swearing (because you're the parson's daughter or chaplain's son or something), you have a few choice options for *cheating the devil*. The same way that spinster aunts are prone to hiss "sugar" and "fudge" (the swearing equivalent of having a Shirley Temple when you really want a Bloody Mary), salty-tongued *wenches* and *rogues* can have fun with the following:

- *fecket*
- *firkin*
- *frigate*
- *fucus maximus*
- *futtocks*
- *double futtocks*

And finally, when the fates are really giving you a hard time, lift your voice to the heavens above and order them to "Go to hell, Hull or *Halifax!*"

PART TWO

Lingua Pira Lexicon

A

adam's ale: Slang term for stagnant water, presumably *bilge,* or that found sitting in the bottom of a barrel. A creatively insulting pirate might say, "Yer breath be havin' the *bilge*-like perfume of *adam's ale, me hearty.*"

adrift: Used to describe vessels or people floating randomly, aimlessly, and powered neither by the winds of the sea nor those of fate.

"So how do ye feel since they caught us *bleedin' the monkey* and cast us loose in the middle of the ocean with *nought* but a *bumboat* between us and the waves?"

"'*Adrift'* pretty well sums it up, *matey.* Now shut yer *ale-hole,* and I'll try not to eat ye in me sleep."

adversary: Fluent speakers of Pirate try to use the most interesting words possible. For instance, instead of saying "enemy," "foe" or even "nemesis," a lingo-savvy pirate might say, "You, me *adversary*, are *nought* but a *poltroon.*"

afeard: Afraid of. "'Tis merely a deadly warship of 68 guns sent to hunt us down. T'aint nothin' to be *afeard* of."

aft: The rear half of a ship, but may also be used by pirates to describe the rear end of a person (that is, "Shift yer *aft*-side, lazy bones!" or "She [or he] has a pleasing *aft*-end," or maybe even, "Nice *aft!*")

after-clap: In modern parlance we might say, "That really came back and bit you in the ass," but the sailor speak of long ago was considerably more colorful.

"I didn't think Pirate Susan would really dump us overboard."

"Well, I dumped her once, long ago."

"Arr, that's a *right* dose of *after-clap*, that is."

ahoy: This word first appeared in print in 1751, but sailors had been saying it for years as either a greeting (similar to "Hello") or as a cry to get someone's attention (instead of "Hey!"). It seems to have stemmed partly from the exclamation "Hoy," which was first used as a way to call pigs and later came into use when calling humans as well. Alexander Graham Bell famously wanted people to answer his newfangled invention, the telephone, by saying "Ahoy." Needless to say, it didn't catch on, but modern-day pirates should feel free to use it as a friendly greeting.

ain't / t'aint: Age-old slang for "is not" or "are not." They tell us not to say it in school, but pirates ain't noted for following teachers' rules.

"So what ye're tellin' me is that *'ain't' ain't* a word? Well, I *ain't* puttin' that into practice."

ale-hole: Mouth. The next time someone from your ship or workplace *runs aground in gabby cove,* you can always say, "Shut yer *ale-hole,*" or if you're looking for a fight, try saying, "Don't be such an *ale-hole.*"

ale-knight: Originally meant "pirate" or "thief," but modern-day *swabs* often use it to describe either a friend or foe who is an enthusiastic imbiber of *anti-abstinence.*

"Yon pirate in the corner's *irrigatin'* his innards some-fin' fierce—he's a *right ale-knight.*"

"Aye, we've dubbed him Sir *Quaffs*-a-lot."

all jaw, like a sheep's head: Someone who is *all jaw, like a sheep's head* talks a mile but walks a minute.

"I can eat anythin' ye put in front of me no matter how vile it be—*burgoo, conjee, loblolly.* They call me Old *Iron* Gut."

"Here then, have a nice bowl of *Scurvy*-O's."

"Er, maybe later, *matey.*"

"Ah, ye're *all jaw, like a sheep's head.*"

all-overish: Just what it says. Sometimes used by boy and girl pirates courting each other as only pirates can. "You be lookin' nice *all-overish* on this eventide." And perhaps after that, "Just bein' with ye be makin' me shiver *all-overish*." And perhaps, finally, after *that,* "I'd like to kiss ye *all-overish*."

ammunition leg: *Wooden leg.* Although it would be nice if this phrase came from the practice of hiding bullets and firearms in *wooden legs,* sadly, such is not the case. *Ammunition legs* seem to have been so-called, because in the Royal Navy, they were allegedly issued to ships along with other everyday supplies such as food, *rum* and ammunition.

anan: The sailor's equivalent of "Come again?" It comes in handy when you haven't heard (or don't understand) what your mate has said.

"Flex yer *bilboe,* prime yer *shag bush* and *look lively, matey.* There be a *veritable* plague o' *picaroons* pourin' over the *rails* seekin' to *spoliate* our blessed state of *arse upward*ness by deprivin' us of our sundry trinkets and *gewgaws!*"

"*Anan, matey?*"

(Note: If you find yourself needing to say *anan* in the midst of being boarded by rival pirates who intend to steal your treasure, you're definitely in trouble.)

anti-abstinence: Any kind of alcoholic beverage. Pirate hosts might say, "Care fer a tipple of *anti-abstinence?* The vintage be a *throatsome* one."

argle-bargle: Unsound reasoning. Pirates might say, "Yer plan be a lip-load of *argle-bargle,* ye *burr*-brained *gaby*." Appropriately enough, in the workplace, this phrase is properly used with people who are completely out to sea. It is equally useful during corporate "team-building" workshops or pirate raiding parties ashore. "That's the biggest load of *argle-bargle* I've ever heard, ye *crumpet-witted gawpus*."

arquebus: A kind of *swivel* gun mounted to the deck of a ship on a tripod or forked rest. Sometimes *swivel* guns had wide mouths that looked like the end of a bugle—good for spraying debris and shrapnel over a wide area. *Arquebus* can also be used to describe the *potato trap* of someone with a sharp tongue. "That's Shrapnel Tongue Sheckie—not much of a pirate, but he's got an *arquebus* of a mouth."

ars musica; arse music: 1) Flatulence, or farting. "Yer *arse musica* be silent but deadly." 2) Brainless babble. "Give yer *arse music* a rest and listen to someone else."

arse upwards: Lucky. "Ye were marooned and yet lived to tell the tale? Ye're *right arse-upwards* then." Pirates who are having a run of good luck might refer to being in a state of blessed *arse-upwardness*.

articles of agreement: Contrary to popular belief, life aboard a pirate ship was not a free-for-all. The *articles of agreement* were written rules agreed upon and signed by all members of a pirate crew. They set out the rules for day-to-day conduct and also spelled out how many shares of treasure each pirate would receive.

asquirm: The act of squirming, either from pleasure or nerves. "The mere sight of that *hugsome wench* sets me *asquirm*." Or, "A guilty conscience will always set ye *asquirm*."

at peace with the fishes: Drowned. Also known as *sleeping with the fishes*.

"Sensitive Charlie's been inconsolable since his parrot went to *sleep with the fishes*."

"How did that happen anyway?"

"Well, don't tell him, but I thought parrots could swim."

athwart: At right angles to. In sailor-talk, this refers to one ship approaching another *athwart*; that is, at a 90° angle. Pirates could also use this to mean "against" or "in conflict with": "Yer scheme be *athwart* o' mine!"

avast: This word was first recorded in print in 1681, meaning, "Stop!" or "Hold on!" It can also mean "Shut up!" or in more nautical terms, "Stow it!" There are many theories about the origin of *avast*: it may come from the Dutch expression "houd vast," for "hold fast," which in English is a shipboard expression for "hold that rope still" (stop pulling it). Or the term may come from the French, Italian and Spanish, which all share the term "basta," which means "enough" (as in "Enough already!"). The Dutch option seems more likely, given that we get many other nautical expressions from Dutch, including "schooner," *sloop* and "yacht."

away: (archaic verb) To go. Instead of just saying, "Let's go to the pub for a quick drink," pirates are more likely to say, "Shall we *away* to a *groggery* for a *modest quencher?*" or perhaps, "Let us *away* to a *grub dive* to *get our bellies 'round* some *victuals.*"

awkward squad: A group of clumsy, ungainly people who lack the coordination or skill to complete a given task. "Well, if it ain't the *awkward squad!*" Also called *gawky squad.*

B

back teeth well afloat: The reader will find many ways to describe drunkenness herein, and this is one of them.

"Sozzled Pete's lookin' well *groggified*."

"Arr, his *back teeth be well afloat!*"

balditude: The state of being bald. "I can't help but notice the *balditude* of yer *noggin*." To be avoided in performance reviews when you're hoping to get promoted or in biker bars when you're hoping not to get killed.

ball of fire: A potent drink. "Have a wee *ball of fire*—it'll put hair in yer ears."

ballast: In the age of sail, if a ship had no cargo, it required additional weight, or *ballast,* to make sure that it sat sturdy in the water and didn't blow over or capsize. Materials used for *ballast* were generally cheap and heavy, such as pig iron, stone, gravel or barrels filled with water. For speakers of Pirate, it can also mean "balance." "He's lost his *ballast* on account of too much *grog*." *Ballast* also pops up in the expression,

"*Look lively* and *shift yer ballast,*" meaning, "Get up and do something."

bandicoot: A large species of fierce rat in India that infests drains. Can also be a genial insult. "What *gawky squad* of *bandicoots* is this?"

bangster: A wild person who follows his or her own law. A famous pirate song supposedly contains the words, "They call me the *Bangster* of Love."

barge: A large flat-bottomed boat used for moving cargo. A word of advice: If you know a pirate named "Barb," you should on no account, even chummily, call her "Barge" as she may subsequently *comb your hair with a three-legged stool.*

barker: A pistol or deck gun. Also a *barking iron.*

"Pass me the *barker, matey.* We're bein' boarded by a boatload of *scurvy buccaneers.*"

"A which?"

"A *barkin' iron.*"

"Anan?"

"An *arquebus,* a boom stick, a *bouncer,* a *broadside*-maker, a *hand cannon,* a *roarin' meg*—oh, never mind. *Ahoy* there, *mateys,* the treasure's in the hold."

barley bree: Whiskey.

barley oil: Beer.

barmy in the crumpet: Crazy. "That's Loony Leg. He's *barmy in the crumpet.*" (See also *seven pieces short of eight.*)

barnacle: A kind of small shellfish that sticks obstinately to the bottoms of ships in great numbers. A *barnacle*-bottomed ship was supposed to be slower, because all the little creatures would "deaden-the-way." Can also describe an inflexible, obdurate person. "Iron-Willed Annie's as stubborn as a *barnacle.*"

barrel fever: Drunkenness. "Ye see ossifer, me *matey* is merely *listing groundward* because of a bad case of *barrel fever.*" (Please note that this excuse will not get you out of any trouble you may be in, but it will at least give the arresting "ossifer" a chuckle as he hauls you off to the brig.)

be: Often used by pirates instead of "is." For example, "The weather *be blashy* today," or "The decks *be clarty,* 'cause o' the *blashy* weather," or even "Barmy Beard *be seven pieces short of eight* if ye take me meanin'." If you are seriously planning to speak Pirate, get used to saying this in everyday conversation.

bear a bob: Lend a hand. "Git off yer *double juggs* on to yer *hind shifters* and *bear a bob. Shiver me timbers,* ye'll be wearin' holes in yer *bumbags* if ye sit around like that much longer."

beard: 1) The growth of hair on a man's face.
2) A useful second component in many pirate names. "Black Beard" was the nickname of the infamous pirate Edward Teach; to make himself look fierce during fighting, he twisted candles and slow-burning fuses into his thick, eponymous beard and lit them. Apparently, this gave him that special "smolder," because he is reputed to have had no less than 14 wives (though whether they swooned from his sheer maleness or the ungodly stench of burning hair remains unclear). Black Beard's fame has spawned a rash of imitators, with fictional pirates often adopting "Beard" as part of their name; for example, Red Beard; Yellow Beard; the famous fairytale villain, Blue Beard; and the list goes on. Unless you have facial hair, the only name really available to you is "No-Beard," and sorry, but goatees don't count unless you want to be called "Half-Beard," "Nerd Beard" or "Geek Beard." Women may briefly consider "Lady Beard," but this has obvious connotations that those not inclined toward salaciousness may wish to steer clear of altogether. Beyond that, just pick an adjective or noun and go crazy. Barf Beard, Crazy Beard, Devil Beard, Fire Beard, Fish Beard, Hell Beard, Patchy Beard, Smelly Beard and so on.

beating the booby: Beating of the hands from side to side in cold weather to warm them. "Don't stand there *beatin' the booby!* There's treasure to be *plundered* and holes to be dug!"

bedundered: Stupefied with noise or speech. *"Avast! Yer ceaseless tongue-bilge has bedundered me."*

beetle-crushing tread: Heavy-footed. Pirates relaxing at home when visitors arrive might say, "I thought I heard yer *beetle-crushing tread* upon the stairs."

before-the-wind: Prosperous. Pirate Smith used to say of the Pirate Joneses, "Them Pirate Joneses be tough to keep up with, on account o' bein' all *before-the-wind*-like."

belay: 1) To tie off a rope. Belaying pins were wooden pegs comparable in size to bowling pins. There were spots all over the ship for sailors to jam a belaying pin, giving them something to tie off ropes to. In seafaring fiction, sailors defending a ship are always picking up belaying pins to fend off invaders. 2) To cease carrying out an order; to stop doing something. *"Belay* that order!" Also, to *"belay* someone's breath," means to kill them. "Of course I *belayed his breath;* he called my parrot *bird-witted!"*

belch: Beer.

belly: The preferred pirate term for either the stomach itself or the general midriff area. "Git yer *belly* round them *victuals!"* (Eat up!) It also suggests earthy, animal appetites (see *belly-gut*), and female pirates about to give birth to little pirates should not be offended if they are described frankly as "big-*bellied* with child."

belly-bound: Constipated ("He's *belly-bound* from enjoying a bit too much o' the ship's cheese."), or someone incapable of thinking clearly and so is constipated in thought ("Yer brain be *belly-bound* today.").

belly-gut: A lazy, greedy fellow. "Pirate Sloth-Beard's a *right belly-gut.*"

belly vengeance: Beer.

bent on a splice: Set to be married. "Making a splice" is a nautical term that means to interweave the individual strands of two ropes, thus making them one. "Aye, them two lovebirds be *bent on a splice.*"

bessie lorch: A kind of fish also known as a *gudgeon.* When pirates, and indeed sailors at large, are looking for a lightweight, all-purpose insult, they often turn to their vast store of silly nicknames for fish. "Thou art a *gowk*-ish *bessie lorch.*"

between-the-sheets chum: Lover; bed buddy. When pirates are up for a spot of *jolly rogering* but are neither in a relationship nor a state of rigorous matrimony, they may seek a lusty companion who is similarly disposed (nowadays a lot of people just call this "dating"). For example, this was once overheard between two female pirates:

"You *bent for a splice* with Dead-Eye Dick?"

"Nay, we're just *between-the-sheets chums*." (See also *ligby*.)

big nuts to crack: A tough problem to solve. "The cannons are cold and the gunpowder's wet? Those be some *big nuts to crack*."

bilboe: An old term for a flexible kind of sword, from the Spanish city, Bilboa, renowned for its fine sword makers and metalsmiths. Fans of J.R.R. Tolkien who are intrigued by this entry should also see *hobit*.

bilge: 1) Foul-smelling water and other vile muck found in the bottom of a boat. 2) The area of the boat in which *bilge* accumulates (from the word "bulge," referring to the part of the hull where water naturally collects). The two most common forms of *bilge* are tar water (having seeped out of the tarry mixture used to seal the joints between hull planks) and drainage from sugar cargo—or worse yet, both. *Bilge* is rightly renowned for its stench, combining the nostril-splitting odor of water impregnated with tar, as well as the corrosive scent of fermenting sugar. Pirates and other mariners find the term incredibly useful, being synonymous with "nonsense" and more generally, "crap." "Yer *sleeveboard palaver* is *nought* but *bilge* water." Also, "Listen *matey,* spare me the *tongue bilge* and come to the point."

binnacle: A wooden case for a ship's compass. *Binnacles* must have been examples of fine workmanship, because a *"binnacle-*word" is a fancy, long word. (See also *sleeveboard* and *jaw breakers*.)

bird-witted: Describes a person of scant intelligence, regarded by fellow pirates as having the cranial capacity of a sparrow. "Barmy Beard is completely *bird-witted*. He wants to git his parrot fitted fer a *wooden leg*."

bite me thumb to ye (I do): An insulting expression that itself describes an insulting action; namely, clicking your thumbnail off your upper teeth at someone in a gesture of contempt. Possibly saying, "I *bite me thumb to ye*!" is an even greater insult than performing the gesture, because it suggests you cannot be bothered to suit the action to the word.

black-jack: A pirate's flag on the traditional black field, as opposed to the plain red-jacks flown by *privateers*. (See also *Jolly Roger*.)

black spot: A black mark on a piece of paper left by one pirate to tell a second pirate that the latter's days are numbered. This method seems to have been invented by Robert Louis Stevenson in *Treasure Island*. It consists of a black card, or piece of paper, given to a pirate by other pirates signifying that its recipient is going to be killed for some wrongdoing or transgression. Other writers have taken the idea and run with it to such an extent that it is now considered part of traditional pirate lore. Sometimes the *black spot* is a splotch of tar or pitch left on the victim's door, while other times it is a piece of white paper with a black spot on it.

black's the white of me eye: An indignant denial when a pirate is accused of doing something wrong. Roughly equivalent to, "I never!"

"There be no *grog* in the pot! Have ye been *bleedin' the monkey?*"

"*Black's the white of me eye*, I did!"

blashy: Watery or foul weather.

"Step careful on them *clarty* decks, fer the day be a *blashy* one."

"*Shiver me timbers!* I've never seen weather so *blashy*. What do ye call this place?"

"Seattle, *matey.*"

bleed the buoy: Buoys are floating, hollow markers that show the location of rocks hidden under water. During the age of sail, buoys were wooden casks half filled with water and used to mark the position of an anchor cable so that other ships would not become entangled in it. *Bleeding the buoy* means literally to drain the water from such a cask, but old *salts* probably also used it as a synonym for "peeing." "I've drunk one too many *mutchkins* of beer, and now I need to *bleed the buoy* somefin' fierce."

bleeding the monkey: Monkeys were tall, pyramid-shaped buckets that were used to hold *grog* on seagoing ships. *Bleeding the monkey* meant illicitly drawing off more than your fair share of *grog*. "That *scurvy spigot sucker's* always *bleedin' the monkey*."

bloody: A curse more or less equivalent to "damn." Fairly harmless to North Americans, but still shocking to some Brits.

"Keep yer *bloody cheese cutter* out o' me cheese."

"I beg your pardon my good man, but you haven't got any cheese, and there's no need to use that kind of language."

blossom: An affectionate term for a bedmate. Feel free to add *briny, hugsome* or any other piratical term of endearment in front of it.

"Arr, me *briny blossom*, thou'rt a *right hugsome* sort o' *ligby*."

"Ye're not so *scurvy* yerself me *long-necked goose*."

bloviate: To boast. "So then I bares me *bodkin* and goes at it *hammer and tongs*. I *belayed the breath* of every last one of 'em, after which I rescued this *hugsome wench* from the lecherous clutches of *Channel Groper* Charlie before stumblin' across a treasure cave of *plate* and jewels!"

"Quit yer *bloviatin', matey!*"

blow me down: An expression of nautical surprise tiresomely overused in literature and cinema. "Well, *blow me down* if *Dimsel* Dan ain't finally signed up fer some remedial pillagin' classes."

blow the gaff: To divulge a secret; to let the cat out of the bag. "A real pirate wouldn't have tipped our *adversaries* to the treasure map bein' rolled up and hidden in me *wooden leg*—ye've *blown the gaff* now."

blowing great guns and small arms: Heavy gales; a hurricane. "'Tis *blowing great guns and small arms* today."

blunk: A sudden squall of stormy weather. "Just when the sailin' looks smooth ye git bonked with a *blunk*."

blustrous: 1) Used to describe blustery weather. "'Tis *blowin' great guns and small arms* in addition to bein' *blashy*—in short, 'tis a *blustrous* day." 2) Used to describe someone who brags a lot. "Yer tongue's flappin' faster'n the white flag on the good ship *Surrender*, ye *blustrous bloviator!*"

bobstays: Chains or ropes used to equalize stress on the bowsprit. Generally useful as one-half of the popular exclamation, "*Jib-booms* and *bobstays!*"

bodkin: A *bodkin* is a short, narrow dagger. Hamlet famously speaks about killing himself with a "bare bodkin," and a pirate *spoliating* for a fight might say,

"Bare yer *bodkin, matey,*" meaning "Unsheathe your sword"—itself an expression so rife with innuendo as to need no further explanation.

bog trotter: An Irishman.

"*Ahoy,* me merry *bog trotter—*"

"Don't be callin' me a *bog trotter.*"

"A *moss bonker,* then."

"I'll settle fer *Jolly Rogue* of Eire."

bombo: A noun that specifically means a weak, cold punch, but modern-day pirates can feel confident about using it as either an adjective or noun, characterizing any alcoholic beverage of inferior quality. "This beer is *bombo.*"

booty: Treasure. If pirates had used the expression, "going on a *booty* call," it would have meant they were off to look for treasure. But they didn't use the phrase, so the point is a moot one, aside from providing a moment of puerile amusement for those unable to get their minds out of the *scuppers* (among whom the author counts himself).

both sheets aft: Very drunk. A cousin of the more common, "three sheets to the wind." Many a pirate has used the phrase, "After more than adequate *irrigation,* we was *both sheets aft.*"

bottled earthquake: Whiskey.

bottom wind: Waves that appear on the surface of water, with no apparent cause. However, this should not stop pirates from using it as a synonym for *ars musica* or *pocket thunder,* or flatulence. "That be quite a gale of *bottom wind* ye're blowin' there, *matey.*"

bouncer: A gun that kicks violently when fired. Lusty pirates often also use it to describe someone who they think might make a lively bunkmate. "She looks like a *right bouncer.*"

bow: The front, or "fore," end of a ship. Or as some *landlubbers* say, "the pointy end of the boat."

box the compass: Being able to rhyme off, either in order or backward, all 32 points of the compass (North; North northeast; Northeast; East northeast and so on). Seemingly, women who could *box the compass* were regarded as sexy. In his 1751 novel *Peregrine Pickle,* Anthony Smollet wrote of "A light, good-humored, sensible wench who knows very well how to box her compass."

brace of shakes: A moment. "Keep yer britches on— I'll be there in a *brace of shakes.*"

brain pan: The cranium. "After a *toothful* too many of *forty-rod lightning*, me *brain pan* is on fire *all-overish.*"

breaky leg: Whiskey.

brig: 1) A two-masted ship with the sails on both masts square-rigged; that is, at right angles to the long axis of the ship. Seen from above, a *brig* would look like this: ‡ 2) A cell or detention area used for holding prisoners on a ship.

brimstone: Sulfur. Useful as a threat due to its ominous cadence. "How does a nice bath of *brimstone* suit ye?" Also handy as a general exclamation, "Fire and *brimstone!*"

brine / briny: *Brine* is salty water, and *briny* describes it. Mariners of all stripes often refer to the *"briny* deep," meaning the depths of the ocean. Affectionate pirates may affix this in front of some other term of endearment for their significant pirate-other. *"Ahoy,* me *briny* blossom" or "How fare ye, me *briny buccaneer?"*

britches (or "breeches"): Pants extending to just below the knee. "Peg-Leg Peg's new *britches* show off her shapely wooden leg to great advantage."

broadside: The simultaneous firing of all the cannons along one side of a gun ship. On a vessel with 32 guns, this would mean 16 cannons firing at once. *Broadsides* were incredibly loud and equally destructive. One tactic involved sailing up parallel to another ship and unleashing a *broadside* into the full length of the opposing vessel. This was risky, of course, because your opponent might be planning exactly the same move.

brownstone: Beer.

buccaneer: Pirate. Many people assume that *bucca-neers* are somehow different than pirates, but the two words mean the same thing. During the late 17th century, poachers on Caribbean islands would illegally kill livestock and then smoke the meat on wooden frames called "boucans." Soon locals were calling the thieves "boucaniers," and before long they were applying the term to pirates as well as poachers. "They call me the barbecuin' *buccaneer*."

bullyrag: To reproach contemptuously in a hectoring manner; to abuse or insult noisily. "Quit *bullyraggin'* him—he's just a *gilpy*."

bumbags: Trousers or pantaloons. "Yer *bumbags* be fallin' down about yer ankles, *matey*. Time fer a belt or at least a piece o' twine." (See also *galligaskins*.)

bumboat: A small boat used to carry provisions, or a small, insignificant vessel. A pirate unimpressed with an inferior ship might utter, "What sort o' *bumboat* be this?" Amusingly, *cockboat*, means almost the same thing.

bumclink: Beer.

bum-squabbled: Baffled. "*Shiver me timbers,* but this tax return form leaves me *bum-squabbled!*" (Admittedly, pirates don't generally fill out tax returns, but you get the idea.)

bunny grub: Vegetables. "Look ye *scurvy* dog, I can tell ye exactly why yer gums are bleedin'—'tis because ye're not gettin' enough *bunny grub*."

burgoo: A vile mash that can barely be called food, consisting of boiled oatmeal with salt, sugar and butter. Ask for it in your local *grub dive* just to see what they do.

burr: A misty halo around the moon before rain. Of one who is foggy-headed, pirates might say, "He's *burr*-brained, that one is."

busking: Nowadays, *busking* usually describes the occupation of string-bashing, street-corner trouba-dours who ply their trade in the expectation that passersby will fling insignificant amounts of pocket change at them. But way back when, it also meant piratical cruising; that is, hunting for prey. "Shall we go a-*busking* today, me *hearties?*"

butter broth: Cream. For example, a pirate asking for a coffee with two creams and two sugars might ask for: "Java, barkeep. Twice the *tooth rot* and double the *butter broth*."

by Gar / by Gum: An uninteresting way of *cheating the devil;* that is, saying *by Gar* or *by Gum* instead of "by God."

C

cabobbled: Confused or puzzled. (See also *bum-squabbled*.) "Tryin' to find a place to park me ship in New Amsterdam left me *cabobbled*."

calaloo: A dish consisting of fish and vegetables. If you're in a fine-dining establishment, try ordering this just for fun. The first step will involve explaining what it is.

caliver: A hand gun; probably derives from the old word for cannon, *culverin*. "Well, *blow me down—ain't* that a cute little *caliver* ye're packin'."

cannonade: A steady hail of cannon fire, either singly or together. *Cannonade* is a general term that simply means a lot of cannons firing, as opposed to the synchronized volley that was a *broadside*.

cantara: A pub or ale shop. "Shall we *away* to the *cantara* for a *modest quencher?*"

caper juice: Whiskey.

capful of cannon fire: A strong drink. "I could use a *capful of cannon fire* to warm me *belly.*"

capful of wind: A light gust of wind. "T'aint a hurricane! 'Tis but a *capful of wind!*"

Cap'n Flint: *Cap'n Flint* was Long John Silver's famous parrot in *Treasure Island.* He was named after a pirate of the same name who had died before the story began but left his fabled treasure map to Billy Bones.

Captain Cork: Someone slow at passing the bottle. "You there, *Captain Cork*—give someone else a *suck at the spigot.*" In other passing circles, *Captain Bogart* is used.

carousing: Drinking extensively, loudly and joyfully with your companions. "Let us find a *wobble-shop* and do a spot of *carousing,* me *hearties!*"

carronade: Full-size shipboard guns might be 10 to 12 feet long, but *carronades* were miniature cannons designed to shoot full-size cannonballs over a shorter distance and at a lesser velocity than full-size guns. The slower-moving shot resulted in many more flying splinters and therefore greater injury to the enemy's crew, which was generally seen as a good thing.

casting accounts: To be seasick. "Don't mind him— he's just *castin' his accounts* overboard."

catgut scraper: A fiddler. Most ships had minstrels on board, and often they included a fiddler. Then, as now, music was a good way to keep spirits up during times of inactivity or hardship. "Call up the *catgut scraper* for to give us a tune."

chafing cheek: An arcane name for a specific kind of pulley on ships of old, but used by modern-day pirates to quiet mouthy mates. "We'll be havin' none of yer *chafing cheek!*"

chancey: Dangerous, risky. "Yer scheme to attack the entire Spanish Armada in little more than a *bumboat* seems *chancey.*"

channel gropers: Get yer minds out of the *scuppers! Channel gropers* were ships that patrolled the English Channel to arrest smugglers. In modern parlance, the expression is often used by female pirates to describe lecherous suitors too free with their hands. "Watch out fer Grabby Beard from the Accounting Watch—he's a *right channel groper.*"

cheating the devil: The use of an exclamation that takes the place of actual swearing. Nowadays, such polite expressions include "sugar" and "fudge." Although not known for their dainty tongues, had they been so inclined, pirates might have burst out with *"Fucus maximus!"*; *"Futtocks!"*; or even *"Double futtocks!"*

cheerly: To do something quickly and with a *hearty* will. A pirate captain keen to motivate his rope-hauling crew might cry out, *"Cheerly* there, me *hearties!"*

cheese cutter: A large aquiline nose. "Proboscis Pete? Why he's that pirate over there with the *thunderin'* great *cheese cutter."* To say to someone, "Keep yer *cheese cutter* out o' me cheese," means, "Keep your nose out of my business."

cheese knife; cheese toaster: A sword. "Humblest apologies, *matey.* I seem to've caught me *cheese-knife* in yer *belly"* or "One careless slip o' the old *cheese toaster* and the next thing y'know they're callin' me Lefty."

chest: 1) A box-like container in which pirates keep *treasure.* 2) The thoracic region of the human torso. In these liberated days of co-ed pirating, the phrase *"treasure chest"* has become a double entendre, which, though perhaps juvenile, is undeniable among a certain set of pirate enthusiasts. You can also imagine female *buccaneers* having the following exchange during the Golden Age of Piracy:

"Did ye git a glimpse into Doubloon Dan's *treasure chest?"*

"Nay, Sister, I was too busy keepin' his hands off o' mine!"

chicken jems / chicken jewels: Eggs. Although it wasn't unknown for ships to keep chickens aboard, fresh eggs were delicacies while at sea. It isn't surprising then that eggs were given this nakedly hungry nickname.

chin grease: Worthless talk. Pirates who have *run aground in gabby cove* might hear their mates say, "Enough o' yer *chin grease!*"

Chips: A common nickname for a ship's carpenters, who often did double-duty as the ship's surgeons (see *sawbones*) since they were presumed to be good at cutting things off, which they often were. "Arr, *Chips*, me left-hand *hind shifter's* caught a whiff o' the gangrene. Care to take it off fer me?"

choke the luff: Having a meal to satisfy acute hunger. "*Futtocks, matey,* but yer *belly* be makin' more noise than a *broadside*. Time to *choke the luff.*"

chowder head / chuckle head: Pirates from Newfoundland may have invented this expression to describe a *crumpet-witted gowk* or similar individual. "Me brother-in-law, Buffoon Beard, is a *thunderin' chuckle head*."

circumbendibus: A long-winded story. For example:

"There I am *dryside* in *daisyville,* when this *clodhopper* comes up on his *daisy kicker,* jumps off all lively like and bares his *bodkin* at me. Thinks I to meself, *Fut-tocks,* and after that *Double Futtocks,* so I pulls out me *cheese toaster* and makes ready to go at it *hammer and tongs,* when all of a sudden—"

"Enough o' yer *circumbendibus*—git to the fight already!"

clarty: Wet; slippery. "You there, Lumber Limb, mind yer step for this blasted *Scotch mist* has made the decks all *clarty.*"

clodhopper: A clownish, lubberly landsman. (See *circumbendibus.*)

cock-a-hoop: In full confidence; high spirits. "Aren't ye all *cock-a-hoop* today!"

cock boat: A small boat used on rivers or near the shore. (See also *bumboat.*) "The only thing ye're fit to command is a *cock boat!*"

cold blood: Beer.

comb your hair with a three-legged stool: A threat of punishment, presumably a violent battering about the head and shoulders with a blunt, wooden object. "If ye don't stop usin' me *wooden leg* fer *whittlin'* practice, I'll *comb yer hair with a three-legged stool.*"

conjee: Gruel made of rice. This is another meal that's fun for pirates to order in fine-dining establishments.

"I'll have the warm arugula salad, the seared fungus garnished with twigs and some *conjee*." (Be aware that if you are ordering in a sushi restaurant, they may actually have a dish called *conjee* which is, in fact, gruel made of rice.)

contraband: Any illicit cargo. Among modern-day pirates, it can also refer to any excellent thing that one pirate is bringing for another. For instance, at pirate parties where one pirate is waiting upon another one to arrive with his *rum*, the first pirate might say, "Have ye got the *contraband, matey?*"

corky: Lively; bouncy, like a cork bobbing on the water. "If ye ever call me *corky* again, ye'll be needing two *wooden legs* instead of one."

couch a hog's head: To lie down and go to sleep. A *hog's head* was a huge wooden barrel that could weigh 1000 pounds or more when full. Hogs' heads were often big enough for an adult to sleep in (though why anyone would have wanted to remains a mystery). "*Dowse the glim, matey*. 'Tis time to *couch a hog's head*."

crossbones: An emblem found on many pirate flags showing two bones crossed in an "*X*" pattern. The classic *Jolly Roger* flag features a skull and *crossbones*. Among modern-day pirate enthusiasts, it is an augmentation of the slang phrase, "I'd like to jump his [or her] bones."

crumpet-brained; -headed; -witted: As well as making pleasant bedtime snacks, crumpets also fit well in front of any general insult that needed a hint of spongy soft-headedness. "Ye *crumpet-brained gudgeon*," "*Ahoy, Crumpet Head, look lively* and rouse yerself" or "Thou'rt *nought* but a *crumpet-witted bessie lorch*."

culverin: An archaic term for "cannon."

curse of Scotland: Whiskey.

cut a stick: Be off! "*Cut a stick, matey*—we're talkin' o' lofty things."

cut of your jib: A term to describe a ship's overall seaworthiness, but also used to describe a person's demeanor or attitude. "I like the *cut o' yer jib*, me *hearty*."

cutlass: A short, curved sword used by pirates.

cutter: A small boat carried aboard a larger vessel, either for going ashore or boarding other ships. *Cutters* were powered by oars alone, or could also have a mast and sails. The rowing arrangement of *cutters* was "double banked," meaning that for each pair of oars, two men would sit beside one another, each one pulling a single oar. *Cutters* had narrower *sterns* than *long boats*. "Let's take the *cutter* and go ashore fer a bit o' *carousin'* shall we?"

D

dabberlack: 1) A type of long seaweed on England's northern coasts. 2) A person whose wits are less than quick. *"Avast, ye dabberlack! Quit sortin' that gunpowder by candlelight!"*

daddick: Literally, rotten wood, and so a person who has *"daddick* on the *brain pan"* is understood to be a bit of a *dabberlack.* *"Absentminded Pete's got daddick on the brain pan—he forgot to take his parrot out of his pocket before he went swimmin'."*

daggerknee: Diagonally. Seemingly too much of a tongue twister for pirates and sailors (who might find it difficult to pronounce if missing teeth), "diagonally" was supplanted by *daggerknee.* One pirate teaching another to play chess might explain, "Nay, me *hearty,* the bishop can only move *daggerknee."* The term also makes an excellent pirate name if you're in the market for one. "They call me *Daggerknee."*

daisy kicker: A horse.

"When I decided to become a land-pirate, I traded in me ship for a *daisy kicker."*

"Don't they call that bein' a highwayman?"

"Land-pirate, *matey*. Land-pirate."

daisyville: A rural setting; the country. "Rural Roger's retired and gone to settle down in *daisyville*."

dance the hempen jig: This expression is a grim example of gallows humor, meaning "to hang" or "to be hanged." A jig, of course, is a traditional highland dance involving a lot of fancy footwork, much of it blindingly fast, sometimes causing the dancer to seem as if dancing on air. And a hangman's rope (not to mention most other rope) was made of hemp—not the smoking kind, but the rope-making kind. "Murderous Meg got caught last week—she'll be dancin' the *hempen jig* soon."

dank: Moist; moldy and smelling like it.

"Yon pirate's got a *dank* and stale-ish air about him."

"Arr, that's Musty Pete."

"*Bilge*-Water Bob's brother?"

"Aye."

Davy Jones' locker: *Davy Jones* was supposed to have been a prominent *sea devil*. His *locker* refers to the bottom of the ocean, especially when describing someone drowned or buried at sea. "He's *at peace with the fishes* in *Davy Jones' locker*."

dead cargo: When pirates hope to find gold but instead discover sawdust, they call the object of disappointment *dead cargo*. "Barkeep! You call this *rum*?! I call it *dead cargo*!" or "Have you met Pirate Kate's new *swashbuckler*? He's indubitably *dead cargo*."

dead man's dinner / dying man's dinner: A bit of food or drink taken when the ship is in extreme danger; any pause for refreshment before doing something unpleasant. "Well, 'tis nearly time fer our weekly pirate's progress meetin'. Shall we catch a bite o' *dead man's dinner* beforehand?"

deck: Platforms laid horizontally in a ship; in effect, the "floor" of the ship. The word also serves as a useful adjective preceding any number of generic insults:

"*Shiver me timbers,* ye *deck*-heap. Lift a limb and *look lively!*"; "You there! The *swab* with hair like a *deck*-mop." (Please note that if you are an avuncular Scottish pirate, it can also be an expression of rough-knuckled affection. "Hoot mahn, ye wee *deck* monkey!")

delve: To search earnestly, or to dig with a shovel. Useful also as a piratical alternative to "Don't go there, girl!"; that is, "We dare not *delve* there, *wench!*"

derelict: Anything abandoned at sea, most often a ship. "Ain't no one aboard, Cap'n—she's a *derelict*." Also, any faculty or ability fallen into disuse. "Bob's powers of piracy have gone *derelict* since he took that job at the Hudson's Bay Company!" (See also *dillywreck*.)

derring-do: Daring exploits in general. "What feats o' piratical *derring-do* shall we git up to today, me *hearties!*"

devilry: Spirited roguery; that is, deliberate and vigorous mischief. "Me *wooden leg* replaced by a cucumber as I slept? What *devilry* is this?"

devil's (anything)**:** Pirates love to put the word *devil's* in front of just about anything that they want to seem naughty, sinful or dangerous. For example, *"devil's* books" are playing cards; *"devil's* teeth" are dice; black and yellow are called the *"devil's* colors"; and a menacing cloud bank is called the *"devil's* tablecloth."

dillywreck: Pirates who are missing teeth, deafened by cannon fire or merely lacking the power of enunciation say *dillywreck* when "derelict" is too much of a tongue twister. "Aye, ever since termites *et* the Cap'n's leg, he just sets about like a *dillywreck*."

dimsel: A body of stagnant water larger than a pond but not a lake.

"Hoy! You with the *dimsel* breath. Ever tried garglin' with creosote?"

"No, *dimsel*-wit, I ain't. Ever tried sayin' 'derelict' with yer teeth knocked out?"

dine with Duke Humphrey: To go hungry. "As the devil is me witness, I thought gunpowder was edible. Guess we'll all be *dinin' with Duke Humphrey* tonight." You may be wondering who Duke Humphrey was and why eating with him should leave people hungry. If so, furrow your brow and read on. Humphrey, Duke of Gloucester (1399–1447) was the youngest son of King Henry IV. Although Humphrey was buried in the graveyard of an English church called St. Alban's, there was a statue or monument in his memory at a different church, Old St. Paul's. Because of this, the walkway at St. Paul's was called Duke Humphrey's Walk, and it was a favorite spot for down-on-their-luck lackeys, ruffians and sea captains to go for a bit of a promenade. Since none of these sorts had any money to buy food, they were said to "dine" on the sight of all the different monuments and statues. And so *dinin' with Duke Humphrey* came to mean "going hungry."

dirty dog: An insult, often overused, but no less excellent for it.

"So, then, Bounder Bob promises to *bent on a splice* with Voluptuous Liz, *swives* her, then *purloins* her *treasure* map and runs off with Cheatin' Charlotte!"

"What a *dirty dog!*"

ditty bag: A bag used at sea for personal possessions. "I like yer *ditty bag, matey.* 'Tis a pretty one what with its bright colors and bold floral pattern."

dockyard mateys: Artisans employed in a dockyard to carve the decorative wooden scrollwork sometimes found at the *bow* or *stern* of a ship. From the gang-like rivalry between *dockyard mateys* and actual sailors, it has come to mean any opponent with whom one is about to scrap. "Let's show these *dockyard mateys* a thing or two!"

doff: To put aside. "I *doff* me hat to ye, Cap'n."

doldrums: Areas of the sea where there is not much wind. Ships that are stuck in the *doldrums* are becalmed, not going anywhere. Also used to describe a person or situation lacking momentum. "Me career as a *privateer* has been in the *doldrums* ever since they revoked me *letters of marque*. Perhaps 'tis time to take up piratin'."

dolly shop: A shop ostensibly selling marine supplies, but in reality, a clearinghouse for stolen goods. "Best git these stolen bolts of calico to a *dolly shop* and convert 'em into *pieces of eight*."

dottle: A plug of tobacco left over from smoking a pipe. Since shipboard tobacco was a valuable commodity, pirates and regular sailors alike would tap the *dottles* out of their pipes when they were finished smoking, to save them for later. Can also be used to describe anything miniscule, dried out or otherwise insignificant. "*Avast,* ye *dottle* brain, quit *whittlin'* yer *wooden leg.*"

double futtocks: Pieces of wood bolted together to form the ribs of a ship's frame, but equally useful as an exclamation of surprise or frustration. *"Double futtocks!"* (See also *futtocks*.)

double juggs: Bum. "Git yer *double juggs* comfy and give us the latest."

doubloons: As well as *pieces of eight,* no chest of pirate *treasure* would be complete without *doubloons* (gold Spanish coins), and a handful was worth a small fortune to a pirate. "Doubloon" comes from the Spanish word "doblón," meaning "double," but what exactly was being doubled remains unclear. It may have been because the first coins to be called *doubloons* were worth two ducats, or maybe it referred to the double portrait of Isabella and Ferdinand that graced the coins. Or it may have come from a later version of the coin, which was worth two "escudos" (yet another kind of Spanish coin).

dowse the glim: Put out the lights. It is another phrase that is both useful and popular in pirate boudoirs. "Let's *dowse the glim* and git between the sheets."

dram: A small measure of alcohol.

"How much do ye want to drink?"

"More than a *dram*."

dredge: To trawl an area of water in search of a sunken object. Also, intense self-examination. "*Dredge* the depths o' yer soul to see if givin' up piratin' is really what ye want to do."

dredgy: The ghost of a drowned person.

"What's the matter, *matey?* Ye look like ye've just seen a *dredgy!*"

"Nay, I had but one capful too many of *caper juice* last night."

drowning the miller: Watering down spirits too much. "Quit *drownin' the miller*. I like to have a bit o' *rum* with me water."

dryside: Ashore. "I'll be *dryside* fer a bit o' the old *fore-and-aft* with me *ligby*."

dubious: An excellent word meaning "questionable." "This *treasure* map writ 'pon the back of a napkin seems to me to be of *dubious* origin, *matey!*"

dudgeon: Anger; temper. "Keep calm and don't choke on yer *dudgeon!*"

duffer: An inept sailor. "*Fumble-Fisted* Fred's a *right duffer.*"

dullard: A slow-witted person. "Well, if it ain't Captain *Dullard* and the *gawky squad.*"

dundrearies: Long sideburns. "Don't trip on yer *dundrearies,* mate."

dungaree(s): Trousers. *Dungaree* is a sturdy, blue denim fabric named for the Dungri region of Bombay, where it originated. *Dungarees* are the pants made from this fabric. "Don't git yer *dungarees* in a knot!"

E

egads: An ancient curse deriving from "Ye Gods!" Although modern readers expect to hear it issue from the lips of errant knights or top-hatted villains, it could just as easily have tripped off the tongue of a pirate.

"*Egads, matey!* What happened to yer *parrot?*"

"Near-Sighted Ned used him fer dustin' the captain's cabin."

el canino: An affectionate nickname for a dog. "Hey, *el canino!* That's me *wooden leg* not a tree stump." (See also *magnificent furry beast* and *tail wagger.*)

elbow crooker: A hard drinker. "You'll like Hollow-Leg Harry—he's a *right elbow crooker.*" (Also known as a brewer's horse, pot walloper, dramster, drinkster, mopper-up.)

English burgundy: Beer.

English gratitude: A punch in the face. "Pull a *stabber* on me would ye? Here's a taste o' *English gratitude* fer ye!" This is another expression of which the first word is the name of a country facetiously used, and the second is a word whose received meaning belies its literal meaning (see also *Irish hurricane, Scottish beef, French courtesy*). The odds are that this phrase originated in a country conquered or colonized by England (or both).

et: (archaic) Ate.

"Last time I saw ye, Appetizer Al and you had been set *adrift* in a *bumboat* as punishment for *bleedin' the monkey.* Whatever happened to Al anyway?"

"I *et* him in me sleep."

F

fair: 1) Beautiful; attractive. "Ye've never seen a *wench* so *fair*." 2) Good, especially relating to weather. "The *mornin' be a proud* one and *fair* fer sailin'."

fair-weather friends: Friends who only ever seem to be around when the weather is good; that is, when things are going well. "Fickle Fern and Gadfly Pat are strictly *fair-weather friends*."

fakement: A forgery or counterfeit. "That *treasure* map carved on old Pine Foot's leg ain't nothin' but a *fakement*."

family disturbance: Whiskey.

fathom: A measure of length equal to about six feet; slang for being able to understand something. "I just can't *fathom* why *Scurvy* Steve's teeth are all fallin' out."

fecket: A kind of jersey worn by sailors and sometimes pirates. Also handy for *cheating the devil* when you've had enough of something. "*Fecket!*"

fence: A receiver and seller of stolen goods. Generally this expression pops up more in crime circles ashore than those at sea, but pirates more than likely had *fences* or middlemen of a sort who they would turn to when necessary. "This load o' *swag* is too hot to unload at any o' the regular ports—we'll have to find a *fence*." Also used as a verb, to *fence*, as in the act of selling stolen goods.

fend off: Literally, to prevent a boat from colliding with another by *fending off* (pushing at) the oncoming vessel with spars, poles or anything similar. Also used to describe the act of repulsing an attack or attempted boarding.

"We've been *fendin' off Virago* Viv and her band o' *saucy wenches* all mornin'."

"You *dabberlack!* When a crew of all-female pirates wants to come aboard, we don't *fend* them *off!*"

fetch (fetching): To *fetch* something means to get or bring. "*Fetch* me that *grog* pot, boy." However, *fetching* can also be used to describe a person (usually female) or pirate who is looking particularly good. "Don't ye look *fetchin'* in yer new *wooden leg* and all."

fiddler's green: When good sailors die, they don't go to heaven; they go to *fiddler's green*. It is an eternal party place where a fiddler plays dance tunes endlessly.

filibuster: A *freebooter* or pirate. "Fish guttin' ain't presentin' the excitin' career opportunities I'd hoped fer, so I'm thinkin' o' becomin' a *filibuster*."

firkin: A small wooden barrel or *keg,* sometimes with a cover, that is used for storing butter, lard or cheese. In modern parlance, it also represents a way of *cheating the devil.* "Don't be a *firkin grumbletonian.* Quit complainin' and *look lively.*"

firkytoodle: Foreplay.

"What's it like datin' Impatient Pete the Pirate?"

"Well, he's got a big *wooden leg* an' all, but he knows not the meanin' o' the word *firkytoodle.*"

first mate: The officer second in command to the captain. Also, pirate slang for one's spouse or significant other. "I'm Blackbeard, and this is me *first mate,* Mrs. Beard."

fish flake: A platform for drying fish. It also pops up as part of similes. "He's got as much sense as a *fish flake.*"

flabbergasted: The state of being surprised by an outrageous or puzzling event. "I didn't mean to *flabbergast* ye by winkin' at ye with me missin' eye— 'tis just instinct."

flats and sharps: Weapons, specifically swords (a pun from the musical term). "Gather yer *flats and sharps* about ye, me *hearties!* They'll not take us alive!"

flea bite ('tis but a): Some trifling or insignificant thing.

"Arr, Cap'n Lefty, yon crocodile has bit yer leg clean off at the knee."

"Arr, Smithers—*'tis but a flea bite* in the big haul o' things."

flesh: Meat. "I'd like a nice plate of *flesh* and *grass*."

flip: A once popular drink made of beer, spirits and sugar. It was supposedly introduced by a 17th-century English admiral with the barely believable name of Sir Cloudesley Shovell, who died when his ship ran aground on some rocks.

"Let's git flapped on this *flip, matey.*"

"I am not your *matey*. I am Sir Cloudesley Shovell, 17th-century English Admiral."

"Well, if ye weren't trying to be *matey*, then why uncork this heavenly concoction o' beer, spirits and sugar?"

"I say, good man, *look lively*—there are rocks off our *port bow!*"

floating coffin: A dangerously unseaworthy vessel.

"What do ye think o' me new ship. I've named her *Holy Hull*."

"Looks like a *floatin' coffin* to me."

flop: To fall flat, possibly on one's ass, possibly not. Pirates and old sea salts might describe someone having such a spill as taking a "soused *flop* in the lee *scuppers*."

flosh: Literally, overgrown with weeds; figuratively, stale through neglect. "The space between his ears has gone quite *flosh*."

flummery: 1) Boiled, shapeless matter charitably described as food (such as gruel or oatmeal). 2) Flattery or insincere sentiments. "To call this scalded porridge I have prepared a 'feast' is rank *flummery!*"

Flying Dutchman: A famous ghost ship said to haunt the seas in perpetual limbo. The story goes that a Dutch captain was fed up with foul weather and swore by "donner und blitzen" that he would make it to shore in spite of God or man. When his ship went down, he drowned with this blasphemy on his lips, and ever since, he and his crew have been doomed to sail the seas, forever trying, but always failing, to put into port.

foc'sle (or "forecastle"): A forward cabin under the main *deck* where sailors lived. Not surprisingly, *foc'sles* have gained a reputation as places where all manner of sailorly debauchery took place.

"Have ye seen the ship's goat?"

"They're tryin' to teach him to play cards up in the *foc'sle*."

fogram: Booze. "Care fer a *mutchkin* o' *fogram, matey?*"

forced men: Men made to serve unwillingly on a pirate ship, under threat of death.

fore and aft: A nautical term for "end to end," referencing the front and rear of a ship. However, it can also mean that one pirate likes the appearance of another pirate in his or her entirety; that is, both *fore and aft*. It can also suggestively describe what may subsequently occur when the feeling is mutual.

"Would ye like to have a bit o' the old *fore and aft?*"

"If it's yer *fore and aft* I'd be having, then *I'm thar* already."

forever more: Always, perpetually. Pirates like this expression for its ominously supernatural implications. "The *Flying Dutchman* is doomed to sail the seas *forever more*. They say it's because her captain died with a curse on his lips, but I think it's really because he was Dutch."

forty jawed: Overly talkative. "Bein' on watch with Babble Beard ain't a quiet time—he's *forty jawed*."

forty-rod lightning: Whiskey.

foul: A generally useful descriptor for anything bad, rank, unsavory or dangerous. "This looks like *foul* weather that be bearin' down upon us."

foul-weather friend: A true friend in circumstances both good and bad. *Fair-weather friends* are prone to abandonment at the first sight of clouds, but *foul-weather friends* stand by you through the most tempestuous of storms.

freebooter: A pirate. Consider this wholly spurious advertisement:

Ahoy, disgruntled privateers!

Tired of pillagin' someone else's treasure for your backer's profit? Consider instead a rewardin' career in the field of *freebootery* at Peg-Leg Peg's Academy of Piratical Arts. Tuition includes Beginner's Eye-Patch, Straw and Feather Parrot, Training Peg Leg.

French courtesy: Rudeness.

"Monsieur *Rudesby* here just told me to peer through his *monocular eyeglass.*"

"That's *French courtesy* fer you."

fresca: An old slang term for rain or fresh water. It raises the disturbing possibility that bloodthirsty pirates might have actually said to one another, "Let's have a sip o' *fresca.*"

Friday face: Long ago this described someone who looked unhappy, but in this day and age, it suggests the opposite. "Arr, *matey,* put on yer *Friday face* for 'tis nearly scotch o'clock!"

frigate: A fast-sailing, medium-sized warship. Favored by modern pirates as yet another f-word for *cheating the devil: "Frigate!"*

frippery: Pretentious, fancy clothing; ostentatious finery. Regular, everyday pirates dressed in *galligaskins* and *feckets* might look at another pirate fussing over fancy clothes and say, "Look at yon *gilded rooster* preenin' his *frippery.*"

frost-smoke: The vapor that rises off the surface of water in cool northern climes. "Quit *beatin' the booby.* 'Tis just a delicate kiss of *frost-smoke.*"

fucus maximus: A tenacious, deep-rooted seaweed that can spread for several hundred feet on the surface of the water. Also used as yet another exclamation of frustration for *cheating the devil. "Fucus maximus!"*

fumble fisted: Describes a mariner who is awkward or inept at handling ropes; also used as an expression of general clumsiness. For example, as overheard between two female pirates:

"Ye've dated Pirate Pete? How did ye find him at *firkytoodle?*"

"Well meaning, but *fumble fisted.*"

fungus: An affectionate if *tough-knuckled* nickname for grizzled old mariners. "Arr, me ancient *fungus,* have another *toothful* of *old man's milk.*" It also works for addressing friends in general. *"Ahoy,* me old *fungus,* what say we lift our limbs out on the town fer a *mutchkin* o' somethin' wet?"

futtocks: The shaped pieces of wood used to build the skeleton of a ship; also used as an expression for *cheating the devil* when pirates are angry or fed-up. *"Futtocks!"* (See also *double futtocks*.)

G

gaby: 1) A conceited simpleton. 2) An adjective to describe same. "Drinkin' salt water ain't no way to keep from gettin' thirsty, ye crusty-lipped *gaby*."

gadzooks: An exclamation of surprise. Nowadays this exclamation usually comes forth from the lips of startled knights, but pirates may have uttered it, too.

"*Gadzooks*, *matey!* What have they done to yer *plank shank?*"

"They called it a decorative egg and dart pattern, but I call it embarrassin'."

galligaskins: Loose, wide trousers worn by sailors.

"Did them rival pirates git the skull with the *treasure* map carved upon its cranium?"

"Negative, *matey*—I hid the skull up the pant leg o' me *galligaskins*."

galoot: An enthusiastic but less than competent person. "Only a *galoot* would bury the *treasure* map *with* the *treasure!*"

galumph: To bump or bounce along. "Ever since Cap'n Strider got a spring-loaded *wooden leg* he *galumph*s around all over the place."

gamey: Bad smelling; offensive to the nose. Overheard in a pirate office:

"Have you smelled that new cologne all the pirates in Accounting are wearing?"

"Eau de *Scurvy?* 'Tis *right gamey,* it is."

gandflook: A fish of the pike variety. Useful in the "silly-sounding-fish-names-to-describe-silly-people" category. "Quit yer useless babblin' ye *gamey gandflook.*"

garfangle: A spear used specifically for impaling eels.

"The invaders have two cutlasses and six pistols each. What have we to defend ourselves?"

"Some *gamey gandflooks* and a *garfangle.*"

"We're surrenderin', *matey,* that's all there is to it!"

gargle factory: A bar, pub or other place of *libation.* "Let us locate the nearest *gargle factory* and enjoy a *modest quencher.*"

gatter: Beer.

gawky squad: See *awkward squad.*

gawpus: A stupid, idle person.

"Did ye see what *Gawpus* George went and did?"

"I heard he got himself elected president o' some country or such."

"More accurately, the pirates in charge got him elected."

get around: To eat or drink. "Let's *get* ourselves *around* these delicious fishes."

gewgaws: See *gimracks*.

ghastly: A general descriptor of unpleasantness. "Yer new skull-and-*crossbones* flag done in floral patterns and paisley and gingham is perfectly *ghastly!*"

gilded rooster / hen / idol: A person of self-importance who struts about.

gilpy: A teen. "Look at the lip fuzz on his face—he's *nought* but a *gilpy*."

gimracks and gewgaws: Gaudy knickknacks made of precious metals and gemstones. The suggestion is of something shiny but in the poorest of taste; in modern parlance, "bling."

"Yo ho ho! What do ye think o' me diamond-encrusted, platinum *wooden leg?*"

"Well, to begin with, 'tis a platinum leg, not a *wooden leg*."

"But aside from that…"

"'Tis a tasteless *gimrack* that borders on being a *gewgaw.*"

give way with a will: To pull heartily together (usually on a rope). "I know it's a life-sized elephant statue made of gilded lead, but 'tis all ours if only we can git it on board. Now, *give way with a will,* me *hearties!*"

glim / glimstick: Light source; candle. One pirate telling another to put the lights out would say, "*Dowse the glim,*" while one worried about wax stains would say, "Don't let yer *glimstick* drip."

gloriously free: Single. Pirates who aren't *bent on a splice* sometimes describe themselves as *gloriously free.*

glum: Unhappy looking. "Why so *glum*, chum?"

gobstick: 1) Trumpet. "The reinforcements have arrived—give a blast on the *gobstick!*" 2) A spoon or other eating utensil. "*Jib-booms* and *bobstays!* Don't eat with yer hands! Have some manners, and use yer *gobstick!*"

gossoon: A silly, awkward person. "He tripped over his own feet and fell right into the crocodile pit. What a *gossoon!*"

gowk: A stupid, good-natured fellow. "Me pirate brother-in-law's a real *gowk.*"

grabbery: Theft. "Let's engage in a profitable bit o' *grabbery*." (See also *haberdasher of grabbery*.)

"That One-Legged Polly has accomplished the *grabbery* of me heart."

"Nobody should talk about their *parrot* that way, *matey*."

grabble: To dredge deep waters in an effort to hook a sunken object; any futile effort to recapture something lost. "T'aint no use *matey*—ye're *grabblin'* fer lost love."

grampus: A whale, possibly an orca. The word comes from a corruption of "gran pisce"; that is, "big fish." (See also *tipping the grampus*.)

granny knot: An incorrect or artless knot made by a *landlubber* whose status as an actual grandmother is immaterial.

grass: Vegetables. A pirate ordering meat and greens might say, "Bring us a *trencher* of *flesh* and *grass* then!"

grog: A chummy way of referring to any sort of alcoholic beverage, but not so long ago it meant cheap booze, and before that it specifically meant *rum* diluted with water. The legend of how *grog* got its name takes a bit of explaining, so you may want to fix yourself a drink and then come back. Ready? Here goes…

"Grogram" was a kind of stiff fabric made from rough-spun, coarsely woven threads. Because it was tough and durable, it made excellent garments for seafaring men who were themselves tough and durable. Sir Edward Vernon was a famous English sea captain who was tough and durable and, furthermore, wore a long coat made of—you guessed it—grogram. Captain Vernon was frustrated by the constant drunkenness among his crew, who called him "Old Grog," possibly because of his tough and durable coat. In 1745 Vernon ordered that each man's daily half-pint ration of *rum* was to be diluted with water and, in addition, had to be consumed in two portions, six hours apart. His men, accustomed to corroding their throats with straight *rum*—a half-pint at a time—didn't like this one bit. For one thing, it made it much harder to get drunk, and for another…well, it mainly just made it much harder to get drunk. Unimpressed with their watered-down refreshment, the crew started calling the drink *grog,* in reference to the captain who had forced it upon them.

Alas, the story just doesn't hold water—the word *grog* had been popping up in print for more than 20 years before Captain Vernon issued his famous order. It first appeared in *The Family Instructor*, written by Daniel Defoe, in 1718. It almost certainly comes from the West Indies, and before that, possibly Africa. It seems to refer to either a sweetened or fermented drink and appears to have nothing to do with tough, durable fabric (though you might argue that any story containing the word "grogram" is worth telling).

grog blossom: Redness in the nose from drink. "That's a *fetchin' grog blossom* that Twelve-Step Steve be wearin'."

groggery: A bar or other drinking establishment. "This be a likely *groggery* to git our *back teeth well afloat.*"

groggified: Drunk. "Don't come home mutterin' tales o' lost *treasure*—ye're *groggified!*" A popular pirate transom-sticker (similar to a bumper sticker) used to read, "Don't sail while yer *groggified*—ye might spill yer *rum!*"

grub: Food, simple but hearty. "Ye look thin enough to fall through a *scupper*. Best git some *grub* into ye."

grub dive: A low eatery. "This be a *thunderin'* nice *grub dive* ye've got here, barkeep. Can I git a plate o' *loblolly* then?"

grub trap: Mouth. "Ye'd best use yer *grub trap* fer eatin' and not so much fer talkin' if ye hope to keep yer tongue, *matey!*"

grumbletonian: A grumbler or complainer. "Whiney Pete's just not cut from pirate cloth. Matter o' fact, he's a *right grumbletonian*." It should be noted that this expression has lost none of its relevance today and can be used freely in the office environment.

"Complainin' Jane's a real *grumbletonian*."

"Why do you give everyone nicknames like that? It makes it sound as though everybody's a pirate or something."

guano: Bird or bat feces valued as an ingredient in gunpowder because of its high phosphate content. Many's the pirate who's captured a boatload of bat crap and considered himself *arse upwards*.

"This cargo o' *guano* wrinkles the *cheese cutter,* but 'tis worth its weight in gold."

"Really?"

"No, not really, but 'tis still pretty valuable."

gudgeon: A kind of fish about six or seven inches long. Also used to describe a well-intentioned but ineffectual person. "Me guidance counselor at Pirate School was a bit of a *gudgeon* if ye know what I mean."

gullery: An episode of deception. "Let's put a wee bit o' *gullery* over on 'em and fool them into tellin' us where the *treasure* lies."

gum tickler: A small drink. "Let's find a *cantarra* and *get ourselves around* a couple of *gum ticklers.*"

gumpus: A fish that allows itself to be caught by "guddling," a way of catching fish with your bare hands. The assumption is that any fish stupid enough to be caught by a pair of obviously human hands reaching down into the water deserves its own special nickname, and that is *gumpus*. Of course, it can also be applied to humans who are exceptionally gullible or credulous. "We told the *gumpus* that Skeleton Island was inhabited by livin' skeletons, and he believed us."

gunstones: Cannonballs or bullets. "There's *gunstones* comin' at us like blowin' rain."

H

haberdasher of grabbery: A master of theft. Haberdashers are, of course, fine clothiers for men, but here the term seems to mean "expert." "Haberdasher" may have been selected simply because it sounds good when spoken aloud before "grabbery"—go ahead and say it in your best pirate voice. "Arr, that Cap'n Klepto's a *haberdasher of grabbery*."

Hades in human form: Hades is of course the posthumous underworld of classical Greek mythology. This particular use refers to hell-raisers and not the fun kind.

"Did ye hear about Cap'n Meanie makin' Pirate Blinky dine on his own eyeballs?"

"Aye. He's *Hades in human form*, he is."

hail: To be from a particular place, or to get someone's attention. "Whar abouts do ye *hail* from?" or "*Hail* that passing ship! We need help!"

half widowed: Describes a woman married to a lazy, idle man. "That's Pirate Susan. She's *half widowed* on account o' bein' *spliced* to Shiftless Pete."

Halifax (go to): An imperative curse. The full phrase is, "Go to hell, Hull or *Halifax*." Seemingly it is an epithet tailor-made for Canadians, since *Halifax* is the capital city of Nova Scotia; Hull is a suburb in Quebec; and hell is what most of us call winter.

hammer and tongs: Very violently. "When Blackbeard and Mrs. Beard have a fight, they really go at it *hammer and tongs*."

hand cannon: A pistol. "Prime yer *hand cannon* and git ready to go at it *hammer and tongs*—we're bein' boarded!" This is yet another phrase that can cause unfortunate misunderstandings on co-ed pirate expeditions.

"Quick now, Polly—both me arms have been blown off—grasp me *hand cannon* and fire it off!"

"I will not fire off yer *hand cannon,* and how can ye even think of that when we're in the middle of a battle?"

hangman's necklace: A noose. "The reward fer *belayin' someone's breath* is to wear the *hangman's necklace*."

harum scarum: A wild, thoughtless or rebellious person. "Ye're growin' up into a real *harum scarum*. Ye should think o' bein' a pirate like yer uncle and his uncle before him."

hatchway: Slang for "mouth." "Unless ye want to wake up with the *spruce* o' me *boot* in yer *hatchway*, ye'll quit callin' me Woody."

haven screamer: A sea gull. Presumably so-called because they noisily hung about seaports (havens) screeching at the tops of their avian lungs. "Them *haven screamers* sound like a flock o' banshees."

having the kick: To be lucky. "Did ye hear about Undeservin' Don? Lost his own *treasure* map and then stepped on it one day walkin' down the street. Talk about *havin' the kick!*"

head: The bathroom on a ship; it was usually at the bow, or at the "head" of the vessel. Nowadays even non-pirates may say, "Where's the *head*?" when *carousing* in pubs or during other social situations. Arguably, in a scenario where you are keen to make an impression of virile piraticality, "I'm off to the *head*" is preferable to "I'm skipping to the loo."

hearties (or hearty): A cheerful address to fellow shipmates. "What ho, me *hearties!*" is more or less the pirate equivalent of "Whazzzup?"

heave handsomely now: Pull gently. An expression often used by mariners trimming their sails, but it has also been heard in pirate boudoirs with more than a little frequency, though rarely uttered in its entirety. *"Heave handsomely nahhh!"*

heave ho: Pull heartily (usually on a rope). The phrase is perhaps most famous as the rhythmic chorus of the well-known sea *shanty,* "What shall we do with a drunken sailor." At the line *"Heave ho and up she rises,"* sailors would pull together at the *"Heave ho,"* but rest on the "and up she rises." Modern-day pirates can use this phrase whenever they supervise their mates in the unloading of something heavy. It is also inspiring to think that the following exchange could have taken place 300 years ago or yesterday:

"Heave ho, me hearties!"

"Shut up and help us with this *keg.*"

heave overboard: To heave overboard; can also mean to simply get rid of something, whether at sea or ashore. "Is that *gaby* nephew o' the cap'n's hangin' round again? *Heave* 'im *overboard.*"

heave the lead: In olden days at sea, sailors determined the water's depth by attaching a lead weight to a rope and tossing it overboard. Then they paid out the rope until they felt the weight hit bottom. By measuring how much rope they'd let out, they got an accurate idea of how deep the water was. However, pirates are more likely to use this as meaning, roughly, "Get the lead out," "Get a move on" or *"Heave the lead,* Lazy Leg—we haven't got all day."

heaving the grog: To throw up, or as the fancy folk say, "vomit."

"Barf Beard's really *heavin' the grog* today."

"Serves him right—the *spigot sucker* drank everyone else's *rum* ration."

heavy-wet: Beer.

heel tap: Whiskey.

hell afloat: A ship or person with a bad name for tyranny. This expression can be used as the nautical equivalent of "hell on wheels."

"Look out fer Bossy Pete. He's *hell afloat*."

"And his bunkmate, Imperious Marge, is *Hades in human form*."

hell broth: Whiskey.

hind shifters: Feet. "Move yer *hind shifters* and *look lively, matey!*" This could possibly be followed by, "Me *hind shifter* seems to've become caught in the jaws o' this crocodile—would ye mind cuttin' it off fer me?"; again possibly followed by, "The quartermaster gave me a new *hind shifter* made out o' water-logged wood—smells even worse than me real foot."

ho: Before it was part of a rap lyric, "ho" was an expression of joy or surprise. "Oh *ho!*" Or it drew attention to something sighted far off, as in "Land *ho!*"

hobanob: To drink cozily. "Look at the two of them, *hobanobbin'* like *between-the-sheets chums.*"

hobit: A small gun, not to be confused with a "hobbit"; that is, an inhabitant of Middle Earth.

"In a hole, in the ground, there lived a *hobit.*"

"Nay, *matey,* tell the story the proper way."

Readers who have already taken note of the entry for *bilboe* may be interested to know that J.R.R. Tolkien worked on the final stages of the first edition of the *Oxford English Dictionary* (though mainly on words of Germanic origin starting with the letter "W").

hornswoggle: Nonsense.

"I'll give ye two pieces o' four, for four *pieces o' eight.*"

"*Hornswoggle!*"

hugsome: Carnally attractive; can be applied with equal effect to both boy and girl pirates. "That Bonnie Anne be a *hugsome wench*" or "That Handsome Ned is a *hugsome rogue.*"

hurleblast: A hurricane. "Cap'n *Arse-Music* over here's got *bottom wind* like a *hurleblast.*"

hurling yer hardtack: *Hardtack* was a dense and often maggoty species of brick-like breadstuff infamously served as shipboard rations during the age of sail. This expression seems to have had two meanings, the first of which makes the most sense to modern readers; that is, to throw up, specifically over the side of the ship. "There goes Emetic Eddie, *hurlin' his hardtack* again."

The second meaning assumes its use as a weapon, as in, "Don't *hurl yer hardtack*!"—roughly equal to "Don't do anything violent!" or "Keep your shirt on!"

I

I'm a Dutchman if I do!: A strong refusal.

"Here now, *matey,* just stick yer head into that cannon and see why she's firin' so unpredictable-like."

"I'm a Dutchman if I do!"

I'm thar: An expression of immediate and eager agreement.

"Care for a tussle in the *foc'sle, matey?"*

"I'm thar!"

Irish hurricane: A dead calm; *doldrums.* The Irish and the Dutch do not fare well in this book, but for that matter, neither do the Scotch, English or French.

"Not a breath of wind fer days!"

"'Tis a *proper Irish hurricane* out here."

Irish tea: Whiskey. This bit of sailor's slang is akin to phrases such as *English gratitude, French courtesy, sailor's blessing* and so on, in which a nation's character is impugned through ironic association with an otherwise innocuous noun.

iron: Masculine-sounding metallic names have always been popular among the pirate set. *Iron* is useful as the first part of many a pirate name suggesting strength or toughness: *Iron* Jaw, *Iron* Gut, *Iron* Skull, *Iron* Fist, *Iron* Brain, *Iron* Leg (cousin of Lead Leg, who can only walk in circles), among others.

iron toothpick: A sword. "Stand aside, *matey,* or I'll run ye through with me *iron toothpick!*"

irrigate: To have a drink; to get drunk. "The next *gargle factory* ye see, let's stop in and *irrigate* the parched pastures of our throats" or "Let's find ourselves a nice *groggery* and git *proper irrigated.*"

Ivan(s): Russians. This way of referring to Russians actually springs right out of the middle of the 20th century when there weren't a whole lot of pirates in sight. But it certainly does sound like something pirates would say. Consider the elegant brevity of the piratese for "Can you show me the way to the Russian embassy?": "Where be the *Ivans?*"

J

jaw breaker(s): Hard, infrequent words; also known as *sleeveboards*. (See also *daggerknee, dillywreck* and *sparrow grass*.)

jaw me down: An arrogant, overbearing, unsound arguer.

"There be TVDs buried on yon beach!"

"What be TVDs, *matey?*"

"Treasures of Vast Dimension."

"Have ye seen these Treasures of Vast Dimension?"

"Nay, but I know that they be there."

"The men what's actually doin' the diggin' ain't seen no Treasures of Vast Dimension."

"That kind o' talk is what I call un-piratical. You're helpin' the enemy when ye talk like that!"

"Stop bein' such a *jaw me down!*"

jib-boom: A piece of wood that acts as an extension of the bowsprit. Part of the nautical exclamation, *"Jib-booms* and *bobstays!"*

jolly: A comely, corpulent person. In this case, the explanation itself requires an explanation. "Comely" means "attractive," and "corpulent" means, without mincing words, "fat." And so to say someone was *jolly*, really meant they were appealingly rotund.

"What do ye think of Pirate Jenny there?"

"She's *right jolly* she is."

"Arr, baby got *stern*."

Of course, today, it is used more often to mean "happy" or "carefree."

jolly boat: Despite sounding suspiciously like the title of cheery children's book, "jolly" was a mispronunciation of the Dutch word "jolle," which meant a small vessel with oars or sails kept in the *stern* of a larger ship—or as it is known in English, a "yawl."

Jolly Roger: The long-standing nickname for a traditional pirate skull-and-*crossbones* flag. It may come from the French, *jolie rouge* (pretty red), after a kind of flag flown by French *buccaneers*. Or it might come from the 17th-century English expression "roger," for "rogue or devil." Or it might come from an oft-heard Tamil phrase "Ali Raja," meaning "king of the sea." The theory is that English mariners would first have pronounced it properly, as "Ali Raja," then "Ally Roger," then "Olly Roger" and finally "Jolly Roger." Ribald pirates may also use it to describe a funsome frolic in the *foc'sle*.

"Care for bit o' *jolly rogerin'*, ye *saucy wench?*" (See also *roger.*)

"*I'm thar,* ye lusty *rogue.*"

jorum: A full bowl or jug of alcohol. "Don't scrimp on the *grog*—make it a *jorum!*"

K

keelhaul: Sailors being punished in this manner would be hauled under the water, across a ship's keel. First, weights were tied to their feet, then they would be attached to a rope that ran across the width of the ship *under* the hull. Then they would be hauled back and forth across the keel while the ship was in motion. In theory, the weight attached to the victim's feet would keep him low enough in the water to avoid hitting the keel itself. But in some versions of the story, this was the whole point, which was to actually drag the "keelhaulee" across the barnacle-encrusted hull of the ship, slicing his skin on the sharp shells of the barnacles—if he hadn't already drowned, that is.

keg: A small wooden barrel. Pirates may well have been the originators of the "kegger"; that is, a drunken bash in which *grog* is drawn from a *keg* for all to drink.

"Pukester Pete's *hurling his hardtack*."

"Don't let him do it on the *keg*."

kelpie: A sea sprite. Visions of *briny* goblins leap to mind upon hearing this phrase, but for sailors long at sea, it may also have conjured visions of lissome, pale-skinned maidens of the deep, beckoning you down into the inviting depths. Kelp is of course a kind of seaweed, but frankly, *kelpie* sounds much better than *seaweedie.*

kintle: A dozen of anything.

"I'll take a *kintle* of yer best *wooden legs.*"

"Havin' a party?"

"Nay, me shipmates keep hidin' 'em on me."

knock-me-down: Beer.

knot-brained: Describes a person who is easily confused. Rope is a sailor's best friend, and any pirate worth his *rum* ration knows more than a few ways to tie it up. But knots can be complicated, and *knot-brained* is a metaphor for a twisting, convoluted thought process.

"Let me wrap me *noggin* around this. Ye're worried about other people stealin' yer *treasure* map, so ye're havin' it tattooed on the back o' yer head where everyone but ye can see it—that's *knot-brained, matey.*"

kraken: A mythical monster of the *briny* deep, sup-posedly of huge proportions.

"That new pirate's a lot bigger than I thought he'd be."

"Y'mean Colossus Charlie? Aye, he's a *veritable kraken* of a man."

L

land ho: A joyful exclamation when mariners on any side of the law first sight land after a long voyage at sea. *"Land ho!"*

landlubber: A non-sailor; a person with no aptitude for sailing. See, for example, the following pirate want ad:

Wanted:

Stout seafarin' sorts for Piratin' expedition. *Landlubbers* need not apply.

lardy: Rich; opulent. "Leadin' the *lardy* life of a *landlubber* has left ye unfit fer piratin!"

league: A unit of measure equal to about three nautical miles (a nautical mile is 6080 feet; a terrestrial mile is 5280 feet).

leg lifter: A strong drink, one that causes its drinker to shiver, shake or otherwise lift a leg. "Blaarrrrrr! This ain't no *bombo*—this is what ye'd call a *proper leg lifter!*"

leg stretcher: A drink, specifically as an inducement for going out. "Strap on yer stump and we'll *away* to the nearest *groggery* fer a bit of a *leg stretcher*."

legs and arms: Weak or flat beer, so-called because it was "bodyless." "Sure I'll go with ye fer a *leg stretcher*, but only so long as it's a *leg lifter* and not some tooth-less sort of *legs and arms*."

lend us a fist: Lend us a hand. "Arr, yon beaver's eatin' the cap'n's leg right out from under 'im. *Lend us a fist!*"

letters of marque: Documents issued by governments authorizing private ship owners (or *privateers*) to attack and capture the vessels of enemy nations. In effect, *letters of marque* were a license to pirate, though other complex rules and regulations were also involved to govern the sale of takings and the sharing out of profit.

libation: Back in the days of ancient Greece, *libation* meant the pouring of liquid, as an offering to the gods. Pirates, mariners and *elbow crookers* in general, however, have traditionally used it as a synonym for hoisting pints in a *jolly* spirit of camaraderie. "Let us make tracks to the nearest *wobble shop* fer a spot o' *libation*."

lick spittle: A fawning underling or *toady*. "Arr, that Kiss-Ass Kevin is the worst sort o' *lick spittlin'* pirate there ever was."

ligby: Bedfellow; bunkmate.

"Are ye and Lusty Gretha *bent on a splice* now?"

"Nay, but each of us be the other's *ligby*."

limb lifter: Not to be confused with *leg lifter* (a strong drink); *limb lifter* is derogatory sailor slang for *landlubber*.

"So I tries to make friends with this *limb lifter* by invitin' him fer a *leg lifter,* because I like the look o' his *magnificent furry beast,* and I says so, but he just looks at me like I'm speakin' *hornswoggle* and then he *hind shifts* it out o' there swift as the wind."

"What do ye think his problem was?"

"I dunno. 'Twas like he couldn't understand what I was sayin'."

liquid fire: Whiskey.

listing groundward: Falling over from drink. When sailors speak of a ship *listing,* they mean it is leaning unevenly to one side, usually as a result of an imbalance of cargo or because it is taking on water.

"Looks like Pirate *Lushington*'s had more than enough. He's *listin' groundward* somefin' fierce."

livener: A morning *dram.* Let's face it, most pirates were not teetotalers, and they sometimes started the day with a *toothful* of something strong. Consider this highly unlikely statement: "After mornin' prayers I like to have me *livener*."

lob cock: A lubber; a term of complete contempt.

"Quartermaster Proudfoot over there struts around like a *gilded rooster.*"

"What a *lob cock.*"

lobbed the keg: Threw up.

"Pirate Chuck really *lobbed the keg* last night."

"Looked just like *loblolly* all over the *deck.*"

loblolly: *Burgoo,* gruel or the like; one of any number of names for boiled muck consisting of whatever scraps were lying about to throw in the pot.

"Scrape that stuff off the *deck* and chuck it in the *loblolly* pot."

lobscouse: A dish of salt meat, sea biscuit, potatoes, onions and spices. Modern-day pirates who want to cause a bit of trouble can walk into any establishment serving haute cuisine and try to order it.

"I'd like a plate o' *lobscouse* with a side of *loblolly!* What're ye lookin' at? Hain't ye got nothin' to satisfy a pirate's palate?"

long boat: A boat with several sets of oars, double-banked, meaning that two men sit beside each other, each pulling one oar. *Long boats* had wider *sterns* than *cutters.* They were often used for raiding parties ashore. "Sir, them *long boats* are a comin' to git us!"

long-necked goose: A handsome man. The under-lying assumption is that any man who presents well "above decks" must surely be "well endowed below."

"Pirate Roger's a *right long-necked goose*."

"Ye'd like him fer a *ligby,* wouldn't ye?"

long-tailed beggar: A cat. If pirates kept cats at all, it was probably during retirement, and this term was a *tough-knuckled* nickname for feline friends. "Quit usin' me *wooden leg* as a scratchin' post ye *long-tailed beggar*." (See also *purring bandit*.)

look lively: Be alert; get active. "Tell Sleepy Steve to *look lively!* The Royal Navy's bearin' down upon us with all guns blazin', and this ain't no time fer a nap!"

loot: 1) *Treasure* itself. "Arr, we got a good haul o' *loot*." 2) The act of acquiring goods through theft.

"That *Lootin'* Lucy seems a *hugsome* hunk o' pirate."

"Arr, they say her *chest* be a full one."

"You mean she has a large wooden box full of *treasure?*"

"Aye."

"Because you might have meant—"

"I didn't."

"But ye could have."

"While yer sortin' that out, I'm gonna buy her a *mutch-kin* o' something wet."

lubber: Someone with no aptitude for sailing; more generally, any sort of awkward, inept or klutzy person.

"What's Pirate *Fumble Fist* like as a *ligby?*"

"Bit of a *lubber* in the boudoir if ye know what I mean."

luff: The action of a slack sail in the wind. When a ship is steered too close to the wind, the sails ripple loosely as they fill with wind and it escapes. It more or less looks like a big rolling wave making its way across the canvas. In pirate and sailor lingo, therefore, *luff* can be applied to anything loose or flabby.

"Hey, *Luff* Gut! Maybe more climbin' up to the crow's nest fer ye and not so much drinkin' *belch*." Or "Pirate Dopey's a *luff*-brained *bird wit*."

lumber limb: 1) A *wooden leg*. 2) A nickname for someone with a *wooden leg*. "Hey, *Lumber Limb*, I'm off to the sawmill. Do ye need a new femur or anything?"

lushington: A drunkard. "Delirium-Tremens Dan can't even open a bottle without a drink inside 'im. He's a *proper lushington*."

M

maggot: The larva of a fly or other insect; an all-purpose insult. This is included simply for being an derogatory term always close to the lips of any self-respecting pirate. The person or thing being so addressed is usually seen as small or insignificant. "Out o' me way or me *beetle-crushing tread* will stomp ye into the deck, ye little *maggot!*"

magnificent furry beast: A dog. Presumably pirates addressed their canine friends much as modern-day dog lovers do. For instance, while scratching a dog's belly, a pirate might say, "Who's a *magnificent furry beast?* Aararararararara." (See also *el canino*.)

maiden: A delicate, helpless and naive woman (or girl). In terms of pirate exploits, *maidens* are useless bit players. Generally, there is little room for *maidens* in piracy, mainly because they don't stay *maidens* for long (for the male equivalent, see *milquetoast*.)

malmsey nosed: To be red in the nose from, what else, drink!

"Dan the Drunkard's lookin' *proper malmsey nosed.*"

"Fairly *quade,* too, if ye ask me."

matey: In a strictly nautical sense, this meant the *first mate* on a ship, but the word quickly came to mean brother in arms, buddy, chum, compatriot and so on. It was also probably used sarcastically to address people who were not buddies, chums and so on.

member mug: A chamber pot (for fairly obvious reasons).

"What is that ye're doin' in me ale tankard?!"

"Sorry, mate, I thought it was the *member mug!*"

merry Greek: A *jolly* companion.

"How now, me *merry Greek!* What sort o' mischievous *devilry* shall we git up to this eventide?"

"I'm Irish, Brother."

"How now me merry *bog trotter.* What sort o'—hoy, no need to pull out yer *cheese toaster*—'tis but an expression!"

merry men of May: Dangerous currents formed by ebb tides. "Be wary if ye fall overboard—those *merry men of May* will pull ye down faster than a lonely *kelpie.*"

messmate: A companion who sits at the same *grub* table. This expression works as well in modern office life as it did during the Golden Age of Piracy, though present-day cubicle *buccaneers* may cause more than a few eyebrows to raise when they ask, "Can I be yer *messmate* today, me old *fungus?*"

methinks: I believe. This is a perennial favorite of people who dress up in the clothes of other eras and throw renaissance festivals, pirate jamborees and jousting tournaments.

"*Methinks* thy *galligaskins* hath been poked through by a bare *bodkin* or perhaps an *iron toothpick.*"

"Stow it! This fake chain mail is itchy, and by the way, your wart is melting."

miasma: Swamp gas; any foggy, swirling or vaporous atmosphere.

"That fire in the tobacco hold has begat a *veritable miasma.*"

"I didn't know ye had asthma."

"I—never mind, *matey.*"

mice feet (to make of): To pulverize or destroy, presumably into small bits. "That's the second *wooden leg* this month that them beavers has *made mice feet of.*"

midshipman's nuts: A bit of bread or biscuit broken up and served as dessert during the age of sail. (Insert your own joke here…and if you know any actual midshipmen, now's the time to *hail* them and make fun of whatever nuts they may have on their persons at the time.)

milquetoast: A weak, timid or cowardly man. Truth be known, this word hails from the 1930s comic strip character Caspar Milquetoast. But the name itself describes milk toast; that is, toast dipped or covered in milk and honey. In the late 19th and early 20th century, milk toast was a popular food for young children or adults who were feeling unwell. Despite its recent origins, however, *milquetoast* has a pleasingly Shakespearean ring to it, which qualifies it for inclusion here. "Ye're no pirate, ye sniveling little *milquetoast*."

Miss Nancy: A prim, affected or self-absorbed person.

"Where's the captain?"

"Busy havin' his nose hair singed."

"Ain't he a *right Miss Nancy*."

modest quencher: 1) A small drink. 2) A large drink. 3) A prolonged series of drinks, large or small, and in fact, anything but modest. For our purposes, it is equal to about one-quarter pint; modest if it's one-quarter pint of beer, but not so modest a drink if it's one-quarter pint of *rum*.

"What manner o' *modest quencher* shall we imbibe today?"

"I've got a thirst fer a *throatsome* glass of *barley oil*."

"Really? I've got me tongue set on a nice *noggin* o' *bottled earthquake*."

monocular eyeglass: Bum, as in bottom; an apt if graphic descriptor for a region of the anatomy frequently admired but all too often sat upon to the exclusion of all other activities. "Git off yer *monocular eyeglass* and *lend us a fist*."

moss bonker: A kind of fish, but also useful as a silly substitute for the proper name of whatever is being referenced, such as a foot, cudgel, Irishman and so on.

mountain dew: Whiskey.

muggy: 1) Hot, sticky weather. 2) Being half drunk. It turns out that almost any word in the pirate lexicon can describe degrees of drunkenness, and *muggy* is one of them. Sometimes it can mean both warmly wet *and* drunk at the same time.

"Bent-Elbow Ben's *listin' groundward* badly and comin' out sweaty and damp *all overish*."

"*Muggy* as an August afternoon if you ask me."

mulish: Obstinate; stubborn.

"*Barnacle* Bill's a *right mulish* sort o' pirate."

"Ye realize that ye're comparin' crustaceans to donkey spawn?"

"I'm not comparin' 'em. I'm usin' each one figuratively—it's called 'idiom,' *matey.*"

"Don't call me an idiom."

"It means—arr, let's just forget about it."

mundungus: Bad, rank, dirty tobacco; also used to describe any rank, vile, stringy or fibrous material.

"Ye call this *burgoo?* It tastes like *mundungus.*"

"It IS *mundungus*—hoy—don't *lob the keg, I* cooked that!"

mutchkin: A measure of liquid equal to a pint.

"Care fer a *mutchkin* of *anti-abstinence?*"

"Maybe just a *noggin.*"

"*Hell broth?*"

"I was thinkin' *brownstone.*"

N

naughty: Descriptive of enjoyably improper behavior. Many pirates use *naughty* interchangeably with *saucy* as a precursor to *wench,* especially at historical festivals where people dress up.

"Thou'rt a *right saucy wench.*"

"Sorry, but I'm not part of the festival."

"Oh, well, how was I supposed to know?"

"Me not being dressed up like a *saucy wench* should have been your first clue."

"Maybe a *naughty wench?*"

"Actually, I thought there was supposed to be a tai chi demonstration here today."

neck oil: Whiskey.

nectar of barley: Beer.

Neptune's goblets: Cup-shaped sponges growing in the sea. Pirates use the term mainly as an exclamation of surprise similar to that old chestnut never far from the lips of Clark Kent's boss, Perry White: "Great Caesar's ghost!" or "*Neptune's goblets!*"

no milk in his coconut: Someone devoid of reason or common sense.

"Batty Beard just tried to catch a cannonball!"

"No milk in his coconut."

noggin: 1) Slang for "head." 2) A measure of liquor equal to about one-quarter pint.

"Is yer *noggin* painin' ye this mornin?"

"Aye, and one too many *noggins* o' *rum* last night is why."

noggin bolster: Pillow. "No wonder yer *parrot*'s always cranky! Quit usin' him as a *noggin bolster*."

no-howish: A feeling approaching illness, but without actual symptoms.

"I'm feelin' *right no-howish* today."

"Bit too much o' the *bumclink* last night, *matey?*"

"It was probably the *curse of Scotland*."

nose warmer: A quick smoke. In the Golden Age of Piracy, this meant a short clay pipe, the glowing embers of which would presumably heat the nose of whoever was smoking it. However, modern-day pirates are more likely to use it as code with one another when they want to slip out for a smoke break.

"Shall we disembark fer a wee *nose warmer?*"

"Those be some *big nuts to crack, matey.* Ye see, they've put up 'No *Nose Warming'* signs all over the place."

nought: Nothing. "Woodchip Charlie's got *nought* but *daddick* for brains."

O

oakum: Strands of untwisted rope impregnated with *pitch* and then jammed between the planks of a ship's hull to prevent water from seeping in. Pirates eating supper at the homes of their future mothers-in-law are *not* encouraged to use the phrase, "Tasty as boiled *oakum*." However, saying, "Your hair looks like *oakum*" on a first date pretty much guarantees that you'll never have to worry about a mother-in-law to begin with.

obtuse: 1) An angle of more than 90°. 2) The state of being stupid or dimwitted. Clever pirates might merge the two meanings. "The angle of yer intellect be an *obtuse* one, *matey.*"

old man's milk: Whiskey.

open throat necklace: A slit throat. "If ye don't git yer pet woodpecker off me leg, I'll give ye an *open throat necklace.*"

outlandish: Bizarre. Another word that serves pirates better than any of its lesser cousins: strange, unusual or for that matter, bizarre. "Instead of an *iron* hook in place o' yer hand, ye've gone and gotten a silver spoon attached to yer wrist? That, *matey,* is utterly *outlandish.*"

P

page stainer: A writer paid by the word, article or book, especially one who pillages dictionaries and thesauri, creating from them a lexical *salmagundi,* which, although it may be agreeable in taste, can scarcely be called nourishing.

palaver: Ceaseless, senseless talk.

"Did I ever tell ye about the time I was sailin' on this *floatin' coffin,* and we was hidin' from the *channel gropers?* Well, 'twas a *proud mornin'*—the old *cheese cutter* couldn't catch nary a whiff of a *blunk*—but then this *bottom wind* comes up and knocks me off me *hind shifters* and down on me *double juggs.* Thinks I to meself, 'Here it is Sunday! This ain't no time fer cursing,' so I *cheats the devil* and says '*Fucus maximus!*' But then, since I'm sittin' down anyway, I reckon why not *couch a hog's head,* and so I do, but when I comes to, I realize I've been *dinin' with Duke Humphrey* and 'tis time to *choke the luff,* so then I—"

"Aw, quit yer *palaver!*"

pantaloons: A fancy way of saying pants, trousers, *bumbags, galligaskins, sit upons* and so on.

panting chum: A dog. "Arrr, me *pantin' chum.* I've found yer tickle spot and got yer *wooden leg* beatin' out a *veritable* drum beat on the *deck.*" (See also *el canino* and *magnificent furry beast.*)

paramour: Lover; soul mate. When spoken after the word "pirate," *paramour* manages to make alliteration seem sexy (well, as sexy as alliteration can be). Sure, everyone vaguely likes the idea of having a pirate lover, but having a pirate *paramour* suggests two untamed souls together against the world.

"How now, me pirate *paramour?*"

"Feelin' *arse upwards* to sail with ye, me *briny swash-buckler.*"

parrot: Widely traveled sailors often kept *parrots* as souvenirs, because they were brightly colored, could be taught to talk and didn't take up much room in the cramped confines of a ship. The popular image of *parrot*-shouldered pirates comes to us from *Treasure Island* by Robert Louis Stevenson. The villainous cook, Long John Silver, keeps a *parrot* named *Cap'n Flint,* and throughout the book he shrieks *"Pieces of eight"* at the top of his avian voice. Although Silver keeps him in a cage most of the time, *Cap'n Flint* also likes to preen his feathers as he sits on Silver's shoulder. In reality, *parrots* are quite smart and can be taught to obey certain commands. It is easy to imagine bored pirates teaching their *parrots* to hop up on their shoulders as a way to while away long hours at *sea*.

picaroon / piccary: 1) A pirate. 2) Theft on a small scale.

"Did ye *piccary* this book from the library?"

"Nay, I just borrowed it!"

pieces of eight: The basic unit of currency in Spain during the age of piracy was the "réale." In the same way that a dime is worth 10 cents, a *piece of eight* was worth eight réales and was also called a Spanish dollar. Minted from silver, by today's values a *piece of eight* was worth about $30 to $35. Since money was valued by the weight of its precious metal content and not its face value, it became common practice to cut these coins into smaller bits (shaped like pie wedges), each one worth approximately one réale. *Pieces of eight* seems to have started off referring to the entire coin but was then also used to describe its wedge-shaped offspring. This is also why a quarter dollar is known as "two bits," because it took two wedge-shaped bits to make up one-quarter of the coin's full worth.

pilchard: A sardine, little fish or other diminutive thing; a term of endearment for a pirate sweetheart.

"Well, me little *pilchard,* shall we make ourselves a cozy lair up in the crow's nest?"

"I'd like nothin' better, me *briny gudgeon.*"

pimginnit: A large, inflamed boil or blemish.

"Have ye seen *Pimginnit* Pete lately?"

"I think he's popped-off to visit his spotty mates in Pimple-shire."

"Oh, you're mean."

pine foot: A slang expression for someone with a *wooden leg.* "Hey, *Pine Foot*, the ship's sprung a leak—come jab yer lumber in the hole."

pine top: Whiskey.

pitch: 1) A mixture of tar and resin, boiled until the two form a thick, sticky mixture. 2) A key part of many similes describing darkness, because of *pitch*'s black color. A good example of this is found in the last known words of the notoriously thick-headed pirate *Dullard* Dan: "Let's light a *glimstick*—'tis black as *pitch* in this powder magazine."

plank shank: Yet another term for someone with a *wooden leg.* It strikes a pleasingly offensive note while still managing to sound chummy. "Hey, *Plank Shank*, the fire's dyin' down. Come stick yer foot in the flame, would ye?"

plate: Back in the old days, to show off their wealth, moneyed families bedecked the walls of their homes with platters and plates made of gold. Over time, the word "plate" became virtually synonymous with flashy riches. The Spanish *Plate* Fleet was a special convoy of ships that transported gold, silver and gems back from Spain's possessions in the New World to her rulers at home. Pirates from other countries knew that the Spanish *Plate* Fleet was loaded with fabulous riches of unimaginable splendor and fantastic worth. The idea of taking Spanish spoils appealed to pirates far and wide. "We can retire in comfort if we capture the Spanish *Plate* Fleet."

plumed out like a peacock: Puffed up with self-importance; dressed in ostentatious finery. When male peacocks want to attract a mate, they fan out their impressive tail feathers in the hopes of getting lucky. Seemingly, pirates have been known to do the same thing.

"Ever since Plain-Dressed Pete met Fancy Susan, he's *plumed out like a peacock*."

"Aye. He even changed his name to Preening Pete."

"He'll not survive long as a pirate with a name like that."

plunder: 1) To raid or burgle for *treasure*. 2) To take *treasure* not rightfully yours. 3) The *treasure* itself. When things are going well for pirates, this word pops up frequently.

"Plundered a lot o' *plunder* then, did ye?"

"We did a *thunderin'* trade in *plunderin'*."

pocket thunder: A fart or flatulence.

"Hark! Be that the sound o' distant cannon fire I hear?"

"Nay, 'tis just Gassy Pete's *pocket thunder.*"

"'Tis that garbanzo bean *congee* he's always *gettin' himself around.*"

poltroon: A coward.

"How's *Poltroon* Pete doin' these days?"

"He got demoted from quartermaster to regular pirate. Seems they found a treasure cave with *nought* but a *purrin' bandit* to guard it, and Pete ran away when the *long-tailed beggar* came up and rubbed against his legs."

popinjay: A target for archery practice, probably brightly colored representations of birds made from straw and feathers. As an insult, the word dates from roughly medieval times and means a vain, foppish person, possibly with a hint of insolence. It is unlikely that salty-lipped pirates themselves would have used this term, but it might have been used about them by outraged kings, put-upon princes, affronted dukes and the like.

"I hereby declare that the pirate, Dapper Dan, is *nought* but a *saucy popinjay.*"

port: If you're standing on the deck of a ship and facing forward, *port* would be on your left. It used to be called "larboard," but somebody finally realized that this was confusing, because "right" is *starboard*, and in high winds and crashing seas, orders could easily get confused.

potato trap: Mouth. "Shut yer *potato trap* before I cut yer tongue out!"

privateer: A vessel licensed by the government of one country to capture the vessels of another country, to sell their cargos and keep the profits. The word *privateer* could apply to either the vessel itself or to any of the men who crewed her. *Privateers* were bound by law to carry *letters of marque,* government documents that more or less licensed them to pirate.

proper: A slang adjective to describe something that exhibits all the expected or desired characteristics of the class of thing it belongs to. "That *malmsey nose* o' yers is a *proper grog blossom*." (See *right* for a fuller explanation.)

proud morning ('tis a): The sailor's equivalent of "What a beautiful day!" It should be noted, however, that "pride of the morning" could refer to whatever sort of weather conditions were wanted for the undertaking at hand. So if pirates were in need of a thick fog to sneak up on some unsuspecting ship at anchor, then foggy weather might have elicited the following conversation:

"This swirlin' *miasma* makes it a *proud mornin'*, me *hearties!*"

"Shut yer *potato trap;* they'll hear us!"

purloin: A genteel way of saying "steal." Its most famous use in literature is probably Edgar Allan Poe's short story, "The Purloined Letter," but pirates most likely used it thusly: "Well, me *hearties,* let's see if we can't *purloin* ourselves some *swag* on this *proud mornin'.*"

purring bandit: A cat. Although dogs seem to pick up all the admirable slang—*magnificent furry beast* and *el canino* (which suggests a masked figure perpetrating feats of *derring do*)—cats get saddled with the likes of *long-tailed beggar* and *purring bandit.* If you remember the principle of *tough-knuckled* compliments, however, it is easy to imagine a retired pirate in his dotage affectionately saying, "Quit eyein' me haddock, ye *purrin' bandit.*"

putrid: Foul smelling; in full bloom of *spoliation.* This is by no means slang, but it demonstrates the creative principle of pirate speak, because it is far easier to imagine a pirate saying, "Arrr, *matey,* yer *hind shifters* are *right putrid!* D'ye mind *couchin' the hog's head* with yer *stump cups* on?" than, "I say, good Sir, your feet smell frightfully bad. Could I impose upon you to sleep with your boots on?"

pyrotechny: An obvious bastardization of "pyrotechnics," here referring to cannon fire. "Them Royal Navy *swabs* is close on our tail. Let's put hard to *starboard* and give 'em a whiff o' *pyrotechny* shall we?"

Q

quade: Unsteady—in any circumstance. In piratical situations, the immediate implication is, of course, one of uneven footwork as a result of drink.

"*Lushington* Bob's lookin' a bit *quade*."

"Aye, seven *mutchkins* of *bumclink* will do that to ye."

quaff: Original meaning was "to carouse"; that is, drink heartily and extensively with companions. Nowadays, its secondary meaning is to drink quickly. "Let's *quaff* these beers and get to the game." For pirates, *quaff* can mean any form of drinking. For example, "'Tis *quafftide*, me *mateys*" is more or less analogous to the modern day, "It's scotch o'clock, guys," signifying that the time of *quaffing* is nigh, regardless of one's beverage of choice.

quatch: Flat. Take your pick of ways to use the word.

"*Ahoy*, barkeep—this *belch* is *quatch*."

or

"*Ahoy*, Sister, what d'ye think o' Pirate Paunchy over there?"

"I'd fancy his *crossbones* more if his gut was *quatch*."

queasy: Slightly nauseous.

"Ye're lookin' green about the gills, *matey*. Feelin' *queasy?*"

"Nay, just *no-howish.*"

queen's herb: Snuff (a preparation of finely pulverized tobacco that is inhaled through the nostrils). To be "up to snuff" was a way of saying that you were either operating at optimum or at least according to formal regulations. "Care fer a snort of the *queen's herb* to bring ye up to snuff?"

quid: 1) A plug of chewing tobacco. 2) In later years, it was slang for the unit of British money known as the "pound."

"Lend me a *quid* fer a *quid, matey?*"

"Tobacco won't cost that much for another 300 years, Mister."

quiff: A satisfactory end, but one obtained by means not strictly conventional. As you might imagine, this term comes in handy for pirates. "So then, we'd run out o' ammunition but we still had plenty o' *treasure*, see? What did we do? We loaded our cannons with sovereigns and *pieces of eight* and fired that at them— tore their sails to *ribbons* and got away with the rest of our *treasure*. 'Twas a real *quiff*."

quilkin: A frog.

"Ye say yer grandma, Pirate Sadie, has a shelf full o' *gimracks and gewgaws* and such?"

"Aye, jewel-encrusted *quilkins* and the like."

quill pusher: A writer or clerk. Being able to read and write wasn't exactly a required skill for day-to-day pirating, but it was definitely useful. Pirates still had to navigate—a skill impossible without knowing how to read and write. On pirate ships, quartermasters were the ones who kept a running tally of how many shares of *treasure* each pirate was entitled to, another job impossible to do if you weren't literate. So although ordinary pirates recognized that reading and writing were crucial skills, they couldn't resist coming up with an off-hand nickname for those who possessed them: *quill pushers*.

quintal: A unit of commercial measurement equal to about 100 pounds, usually in barrels.

"Ye look like ye could use a *mutchkin* o' *brownstone, matey!*"

"A *quintal's* more like it."

R

ragged arsed: Tattered; worn out; haphazard.

"Well, Cap'n, here's the bloodthirsty pirate crew we've been able to muster."

"What d'ye mean? That one's got his eye patch coverin' his good eye. The one next to him's got a horseshoe instead of a hook. And the one on the end's got both his legs, but he's pulled one up behind him and strapped a fake *wooden leg* onto his knee. What sort of *ragged-arsed awkward squad* is this?

rails: *Rails* are the portions of a ship's hull that rise up above the deck, helping to prevent sailors from sliding overboard. Invading pirates boarding a ship are invariably described as "pouring over the *rails.*"

raise the flag of defiance: To have a booze-up. Nowadays we say "raise a little hell, raise a little hell, raise a little hell," but when pirates wanted to cut loose with the help of their old mate, alcohol, it was more apt to sound like this: "We're off in quest of a *groggery* to *raise the flag of defiance.*"

ramrod: A handheld pole with a swab of rags on one end, used for packing or "ramming" gunpowder into cannons. Also, among earthy female pirates, it makes a salacious metaphor for a spirited bunkmate.

"How's yer new pirate *paramour?*"

"I call him *Ramrod Roger!*"

ransack: To pillage or burgle, by tearing things apart. "We *ransacked* the governor's fortress and *plundered* lots o' *swag.*"

red hot balls: Cannonballs heated up until they are red hot and then fired at the enemy. Also useful as a quaint curse. "*Red hot balls!* Ye startled me there."

ribald: Jocularly lewd. In general, the *blustrous* sorts who enjoy talking like pirates can safely be described as *ribald.* "Let us find ourselves some several *saucy wenches* and see what *ribald* adventures we might have."

ribbons: Tatters. Mainly useful as a threat. "Move another step, and we'll cut ye to *ribbons!*"

rig of a ship: A ship's *rigging* is the complex arrangement of ropes that sailors use to raise, lower or otherwise adjust their sails. The *rig of a ship* refers to one of many different ways that ships can be rigged. Among pirates and sailors, though, it finds favor as a way to say that you like someone's attitude or way of doing things. "I like the *rig of* yer *ship!*" (See also *cut of your jib.*)

right: Slang for something that is exemplary; a precursor to a metaphor. Sailors and *landlubbers* alike often use *right* to describe something that is exemplary of its kind; that is, it has all the qualities that you would expect of whatever the thing is. If you see a sailor whose red nose presents a stereotypical picture of inebriation, you could say, "That's a *right grog blossom* ye're sportin' there, *matey.*" It can also mean *veritable,* or as we say, "virtually," when used in front of a metaphor. For instance, of a shipmate who is prominently flatulent, you might say, "That's a *right* symphony of *arse musica* yer fartin' up there, *matey.*"

ripper: 1) Something that is, itself, excellent. "Yer *wooden leg* with a gun in it is a real *ripper!*" 2) An adjective to describe an excellent thing, as in, "You've got a *wooden leg* with a gun in it? That's *ripper!*"

roaring meg: "Roaring Meg" was the name given to a famous cannon that was used in the English civil war, so-called because of the loud sound it made when fired. As a slang term, *roaring meg* refers to anything loud, excellent or both.

"Hey, ye're datin' Magnificent Megan, aren't ye? What's that like?"

"I call her *Roaring Meg.*"

Or, less suggestively:

"I like yer new ship."

"Aye, she's a real *roarin' meg,* ain't she?"

roger: To have sex. This use of the word actually dates back to the 1650s and provides lots of opportunity for innuendo when used as part of any lewd or lascivious pun involving the classic pirate skull and *crossbones,* namely, the *Jolly Roger.*

"Have you met Pirate Peggy's new *paramour?*"

"Aye, I'd like to jump his *crossbones.*"

"He looks like he'd be quite a *jolly roger,* doesn't he?"

rogue: A rascally fellow of dastardly (though some might say "appealingly impudent") tendencies. Also known as bounders, cads and ne'er-do-wells. Co-ed pirating situations are usually populated by *rogues* and *wenches,* each taking pleasure in so-addressing the other.

"You're a *right* handsome *rogue.*"

"And you're a *proper hugsome wench.*"

rot gut: Whiskey.

roundly: Quickly. "Strap yer *cutlass* on *roundly, matey*—they're comin' over the *rails* even as we speak."

rover: A pirate.

"I'm what ye might call a *rover* of the seas."

"You mean a pirate?"

"Arr, that's right. A *buccaneer,* a *freebooter,* a *picaroon,* a *swashbuckler*—"

"Quit yer *tongue bilge.* I understood ye the first time."

"No need to be a *rudesby* about it!"

rudesby: A rude person. (See *rover*).

rum: An alcoholic drink distilled from molasses or sugar cane. *Rum* was the pirate drink of preference mainly because it was plentiful. The Caribbean, where many pirates were active, was home to huge sugar-cane crops. *Rum* was an immensely popular drink the world over, and it was often traded as a commodity. Pirate vessels and ships of the Royal Navy adopted the practice of distributing a daily ration of *rum* to all sailors. This was probably a reward, partly to ensure compliance and partly because maintaining a supply of potable water was extremely difficult.

run aground in addle cove: A ship that has *run aground* is stuck on either submerged rocks or, more embarrassingly, the shore—it's not a good thing. Someone who has *run around in addle cove* may be merely stumped, completely deranged or perhaps just impaled on the horns of dilemma.

"Ever since that cannon ball fell on his head, old Baffle Beard's been *run aground in addle cove.*"

"Arr. Yesterday I caught him tryin' to teach his *parrot* how to navigate."

run aground in gabby cove: When someone has *run aground in gabby cove*, it means they have fallen into a stream of ceaseless talking. "Arr, yon yammerin' pirate goes by the name o' *Bloviatin'* Bob—he's in a permanent state o' bein' *run aground in gabby cove*."

S

sail in the same boat: To be of similar principles, goals or outlooks.

"How do ye feel about *woolding* as a means of torture?"

"I feel fine about it—just don't ask me to watch."

"You and me *sail in the same boat, matey.* I like the *rig of yer ship.*"

sailor's blessing: Swearing, presumably in the most foul-mouthed manner possible. The term joins a list of other greats, all of which are precisely the opposite of what they suggest. (See also *English gratitude, Irish hurricane, Irish tea, Scottish beef.*)

salmagundi: 1) A dish of minced meat and seafood arranged in rows on lettuce and drizzled with dressing. 2) A mish-mash of anything. *Salmagundi* is famous for supposedly being served on pirate ships where the cook might put in whatever sort of fish or seafood was available. Although there are many different theories on how the name evolved, many are convinced that it was eventually bastardized into the name of the title character in the popular children's nursery rhyme, "Solomon Grundy":

Solomon Grundy,

Born on a Monday,

Christened on Tuesday,

Married on Wednesday,

Took ill on Thursday,

Grew worse on Friday,

Died on Saturday,

Buried on Sunday.

That was the end of Solomon Grundy.

salt / old salt: A weather-beaten sailor. We can only assume that since seawater is salty, *old salts* had been at sea so long that they themselves had become salty. "*Avast,* me *old salt*; ye'll be wantin' to lay off the *old man's milk.*"

sangaree: A reddish-colored drink of the south Indies made from port or Madeira, water, lime juice, sugar and nutmeg, perhaps with some other sort of alcohol mixed in; we call its modern equivalent "sangria." It takes its name from the French word "sang," meaning "blood," because of its bright red color. "Arr, that was a gory battle—the decks look like we had a *sangaree* party on 'em."

saucy: Pleasingly impudent. Initially, it simply meant "lip," or as modern speakers would say, "attitude." But down through the years, many people, pirates and otherwise, have come to see someone who is *saucy* as being adorably impertinent. And for the most part, nowadays, one almost always hears it in front of the word *wench*.

"Ye're a *saucy wench,* ye are."

"Look, I told you already, I'm not part of the pirate festival."

"Fine, then I'll just call ye *saucy.*"

(Hint: Sometimes the best way to meet a *wench* is not to call her one.)

savage as a meat axe: Ravenously hungry. "I'm *savage as a meat axe*. I best *get around* some o' that *salmagundi.*"

sawbones: Popular slang, meaning "doctor." However, pirate ships rarely had actual doctors on board, so the job usually fell to the ship's carpenter. Because carpenters were presumably good at sawing things off, surely their skill extended to amputating limbs. And considering the state of medical science during the Golden Age of Piracy, your chances were as good with a carpenter as a surgeon.

"Hoy, you there, *sawbones*, I need ye to cut me leg off."

"You mean the wooden one?"

"Aye, the boys used some kind o' tree sap to stick it to me knee joint and now I can't git it off."

scandal broth: Surprisingly, this slang term for a popular beverage refers not to alcohol but to tea. The idea was that nattering gossips would exchange rumors and innuendo over steaming cups of tea, or *scandal broth*. Anyone who wonders why tea is popping up in a book about pirates would do well to remember that Bartholomew Roberts (a.k.a. "Black Bart"), one of the most successful and wantonly cruel pirates of his age, liked nothing more than taking a cuppa in his cabin.

"Did ye enjoy yer mornin' session o' *wooldin'* and *keelhaulin'*, Black Bart?"

"Indeed, my good man. Go flog yourself and then join me for a cup of *scandal broth*."

Scotch mist: A soaking rain. Another fine example of the way that primarily English pirates could turn something as mundane as rain into a xenophobic insult.

"Havin' trouble gettin' yer *nose warmer* lit?"

"Arr, 'tis this *bloody Scotch mist*."

Scottish beef: Fish. (See *Scotch mist* for the reason behind this name. Other terms include *Irish hurricane* and *French courtesy,* among others.)

scoundrel: Someone devoid of every principle of honor; a term freely applied to pirates of all stripes: sea, river, space and so on.

"At first I thought Selfish Steve liked me fer the pirate that I am, but now I realize that he just wanted to git a look at me *treasure* chest."

"He's a *scoundrel!*"

scour the seas: 1) To infest the ocean as a pirate. 2) To search intently for something.

"I'm *scourin' the seas* fer a shipful of *treasure.*"

"Wouldn't it be more efficient to simply hang around near ports and trading posts where richly laden ships might be putting in?"

"You really take all the fun out of piratin', you know that?"

scrimshaw: Intricate carving on the surface of whale-bone, whale teeth or the tusk of any other sea creature. The Golden Age of Piracy lasted from roughly 1680 to 1730, but the word *scrimshaw* does not appear until the mid to late 1800s. However, it is so pungently piratical sounding that modern-day *wenches* and *rogues* should feel free to use it as they see fit.

"Sufferin' *scrimshaw!*" Or:

"They call me Captain *Scrimshaw.*"

"I'd feel better if they called you a dentist, Dr. Payne."

The origins of *scrimshaw* are hotly debated. One possible source is the French word, *escrimer*, which means "to fight with a sword," and so to make flourishing motions with a pointy object, presumably similar to the activity of carving.

scruff: Barnacles and other detritus adhering to the bottom of a boat. Nowadays, *scruffy* can describe someone who is unshaven, shabbily dressed or of generally raggedy appearance. So it isn't a far stretch to imagine sailors and pirates so unkempt that they appeared to have barnacles and other detritus stuck to their faces or other parts. The following was once overheard in a female pirate locker room.

"That Dapper Dan is my cuppa tea!"

"*Scruffy* Steve is more my type—his *parrot* says nice things to me."

scumgullion: Whiskey.

scuppers: Round openings in the hull of a ship just above deck level that allow water to run off the deck. To modern pirates, it is most useful as a rough equivalent of *gutters*. "Git yer mind out o' the *scuppers, matey.* Me relationship with Luscious Susan is perfectly platonic." (Though it is difficult to the think of a word less likely to pass a pirate's lips than "platonic.") *Scuppers* is also famously referenced in the traditional sea shanty, "What shall we do with a drunken sailor?"; the answer to which, among other things, is to "put him in the *scuppers* with a hosepipe on him, early in the morning" ("early" is pronounced "earl-eye").

The other things to do with a drunken sailor early in the morning: put him in the *bilge* and make him drink it; spray him in whiskey and light him on fire; hit him on the head with a broken hammer; hang him from the sails until his eyeballs fall out; shave his *belly* with a rusty razor.

scurvy: Scurvy, of course, was the disease contracted by mariners on long voyages when they did not consume enough fresh fruits or vegetables. Its unpleasant symptoms included bleeding, spongy gums and bleeding under the skin. The name for the disease may come from the old expression "scurf," which meant "scab," and there's a good chance that sailors knew perfectly well they were calling each other "scabby." *Scurvy* can also be loosely used to mean dastardly, naughty, salty, *saucy,* unpalatable and so on.

sea: The ocean. Saying "sea" before anything gives it a salty nautical flavor. "*Avast,* ye *sea* dog, lay down yer arms" or "Come and give yer pirate grandpa a hug ye wee *sea* turnip" or "Thou'rt a *right sea* goddess" (which, in hopeful pirate dreams, is followed by, "Ye can bury yer *treasure* on me beach anytime, *matey*").

sea devil: A kind of fish, but also a generally useful insult describing a foe who is unusually persistent or aggressive.

"This is the seventh time that *Spleenful Ivan's* attacked us today!"

"Arr, he's a *right sea devil*...did I mention that I accidentally boiled his *parrot* in a samovar?"

sea wolves: Pirates. It is difficult to tell who coined this macho term for pirates: the authorities chasing them, the women who fantasized about them, or the pirates themselves.

seven pieces short of eight: If you haven't read the entry for *pieces of eight* yet, you should. The same way that *landlubbers* say someone is "a few sandwiches short of a picnic," pirates say someone is *seven pieces short of eight*, meaning that the person in question is a long way from being all there. "See yon pirate runnin' naked through the mosquitoes? That's Nutty Bob—he's *seven pieces short of eight* if ye take my meanin'."

shack rag: A lazy shiftless fellow. "See *Half-Widowed* Helen over there? She's married to *Shack Rag* Charlie."

shag bush: A pistol or *arquebus*. Noted for causing confusion on co-ed pirate expeditions.

"Pass me yer *shag bush,* Sister."

"Beggin' yer pardon, Brother, but we've just met."

"Look, *matey,* the navy's boardin' us, and a *hand cannon* or a *bouncer'd* come in handy right about now."

"I will not bounce anyone's *hand cannon,* and I find yer tone suggestive."

"Arr, 'tis suggestive of us bein' boarded by hostile sailors! Now git yer mind out o' the *scuppers* and give me a gun!"

shake yer shank: Get a move on; hustle your butt and so on.

shakey: Undependable. "Ye left Thirsty Bob to guard the *grog?* As his name suggests, he's just a little *shakey* in that department."

shank: Slang for "leg." "Shift yer *shank* and *look lively, matey.*"

shanty: A rhythmic song, sung at sea by a group of men as they *heave* together on ropes to raise sails or other heavy burdens. (See also *heave ho* and *scupper.*)

"*Ahoy* there, minstrel! Lead us in a sea *shanty.*"

"What Shall We Do With a Drunken Sailor?"

"How about the other one—What *Devilry* Can We Inflict on a *Groggified* Mariner? It goes to the same tune."

shebeen: A drinking establishment of enjoyably low character.

"Shall we find ourselves a *gargle factory?*"

"Too respectable."

"Maybe a *wobble shop?*"

"Try one lower."

"A *groggery* then?"

"Scrape the bottom, *matey.*"

"A *shebeen!*"

"Now ye're talkin'!"

shift yer ballast: Get off your ass; lift a leg; do something and so on.

"*Shift yer ballast, matey.* There's ropes that need a haulin'."

"Haul on THIS, *matey!*"

Shiver me timbers!: Along with *Arr* and *matey*, this expression of surprise is never far from the lips of pirates in fiction and film. It is easy to imagine that the timbers being shivered are those of a boat that has just struck a rock, or perhaps even the timber in a pirate's *wooden leg*. Although they both make sense, neither of these explanations appear to be true. "Timbers!" was a real exclamation of surprise (like "Goodness!" or "Heavens!") but with no specific meaning. The word first appears in the popular song,

"Poor Jack," by the English lyricist and composer Charles Dibdin (1745–1814). In the song, Dibdin describes a long, rambling sermon by a ship's chaplain. As a metaphor for the chaplain's tangled sentences and fancy words, Dibdin uses the image of a coil of rope, knotted and twisted around itself:

> I heard our good chaplain palaver one day
>
> About souls, heaven, mercy and such;
>
> And, my timbers! what lingo he'd coil and belay;
>
> Why, 'twas just all as one as High Dutch;

A few years later, in 1834, sailor-turned-novelist Captain Frederick Marryat appears to have invented the phrase "Shiver my timbers" in his book *Jacob Faithful*—and so was born a popular saying that, to this day, stubbornly refuses to actually mean anything.

sit upons: Trousers.

"I like the dashin' cut of yer *sit upons, matey.*"

"Me whats?"

"Yer *galligaskins.* Yer *bumbags.* What's the matter? Don't ye parley English?"

skirting the cannonballs: The inclusion of the words "skirt" and "balls" in this expression can be no coincidence, for it describes an excellent maneuver in which a boatload of female pirates swoop in and take the *treasure* by virtue of not involving themselves in the cannon fire and sword banging of the men. "While the boys was busy firin' *broadsides* at each other and *swashbucklin'* and the like, me and my *wenches skirted the cannonballs* and made off with the *treasure*."

slack jaw: Lip; sass; sauciness. A redundant pirate *buccaneer* might say, "Enough o' yer *saucy slack jaw*."

sleeveboard: A hard word to pronounce; that is, hard to pronounce for sailors and pirates, any of whom might be missing teeth or tongues due to *scurvy*, battle, torture and the like. Also called a *jaw breaker*. If you encounter a s*leeveboard,* the correct course of action is to come up with a replacement word that is both easier to pronounce and roguishly poetical, such as *daggerknee, dillywreck* and *sparrow grass*.

sleeveless: Inadequate; weak.

"We missed ye on pillagin' detail yesterday."

"I had to take me new *parrot* back to the shop. Turns out the *scurvy parrot* merchant had just nailed him to the perch and sold me an ex-*parrot*."

"What sort of *sleeveless* excuse is that?"

(Note: In a work of this nature, more than one dead parrot joke is bound to pop up.)

slippery: As well as describing a surface or object that lacks traction as a result of being wet, *slippery* can also describe a *sleeveless* line of reasoning; that is, one which is unsound or weak.

"Let me git me wits around this plan of yourn. Ye want to just arbitrarily draw yer own *treasure* map, put a big '*X*' on it and then go off and dig, assumin' there'll be *treasure* there. That's a *slippery* line o' thought at best, *matey*. Why don't ye start piratin' from home too and see how that works out?"

sloop: A single-masted ship. Hollywood always portrays pirates as sailing about in two- or even three-masted schooners, but the majority of pirating was done in single-masted *sloops*.

sly boots: A pirate or person who, on the outside, seems to be a *crumpet-witted gaby* or maybe even *seven pieces short of eight,* but in reality, hides a cunning nature behind a gormless facade.

"The new quartermaster seems like a bit of a *gawpus*."

"Ye mean Murderin' Machiavelli? Nay, he's a *sly boots*, that one is."

smart: Intelligent; active. "Look *smart* ye *gawky squad* o' *lubbers*."

smeller: Nose.

"*Egads!* Yon pirate's got a big *smeller*."

"That's Proboscis Pete, but he prefers it if ye call him Aquiline Al."

smiter: A sword. "Smite" is an archaic English word meaning "to hit." To smite someone a mighty blow means you've struck the person with great force. To call a sword a *smiter* suggests a violent battle of little finesse and much bloodshed. "Git yer *smiter* out, *matey*—them barbarian pirates are swarmin' over our *rails*."

smuggle: To transport contraband or hidden goods, often concealed in cunning ways. Pirates did the stealing, but they often relied on middlemen or *fences* to convert their goods into cash. After the *fence* had taken possession of the goods, *smugglers* might ship the ill-gotten gains from point A to point B, often using ingenious methods of concealment. "The port authorities kept uncorkin' Wiley Bob's hollow *wooden leg,* but they could never find anything. Then they figured out that he was actually *smugglin'* hollow *wooden legs*."

snarl knot: A stubborn or badly tied knot that is hard to loosen. It can also describe a problem that is difficult to overcome or solve. "So ye taught yer *parrot* to say the location of the *treasure* and then lost him in a poker game—that be a *right snarl knot, matey*." (See also *big nuts to crack*.)

sneezer: A stiff gale of wind. "What a *sneezer*! It's torn yer *Jolly Roger* a new eye socket!"

snorter: Anything large or exceptional. "Have ye seen *Gewgaw* Gord's new pirate pendant? 'Tis a gold skull and *crossbones* encrusted in gemstones—'tis a *snorter*."

snout: Nose.

"Keep yer *snout* out o' me business, *matey.*"

"Pardon?"

"Keep yer *cheese cutter* out o' me cheese—yer *smeller* out o' me smellin'.'"

"Oh. Why didn't ye just say so?"

snudge snout: A dirty person.

"That's Slovenly Sue. She's a *proper snudge snout.*"

"Pigpen Pete's her *paramour,* ain't he?"

sparrow grass: Presumably, "asparagus" was too much of a *sleeveboard* for many folk, and so *sparrow grass* was coined.

"Some baked *sparrow grass* would be *right throatsome* just about now—maybe brushed with minced garlic, a dash of pepper and just a hint of rosemary."

"Talkin' like that, the only thing around here I'm callin' Rosemary is you, *matey.*"

spewing the oakum: To throw up (with the suggestion of chunky texture; see *oakum*).

"Up-Chuck Charlie's sure livin' up to his name."

"Arr, he's really *spewin' the oakum.*" (See also *casting accounts; heaving the grog; hurling your hard tack.*)

spigot sucker: Drunkard.

"*Malmsy-Nosed* Ned's been *bleedin' the monkey* again."

"Aye, that *spigot sucker*'s *forever purloinin'* an extra *toothful* of *grog*."

spleenful: Bad-tempered.

"That's Sourpuss Patty. She's a *right spleenful* sort o' pirate."

"Might make a good mate fer Dour Dan."

splicing the main brace: An extra ration of *grog* in bad weather after severe exertion. During the age of sail, the main brace was a fixed point that pulleys or ropes were attached to for the purpose of trimming the mainsail. To splice it would have meant to reinforce it or attach it firmly, so the idea of having an extra capful of *grog* as a restorative after hard work makes perfect sense. "It's been a day of rough weather, me *hearties*. Time to *splice the main brace*."

splinter toe: An offhand nickname for someone with a *wooden leg*. "Ready yer tweezers, mates. Here comes *Splinter Toe*."

spoils: *Treasure* taken from someone else. "Back from yer raidin' expedition? Let's see the *spoils!*"

spoliate / spoliation / spoliator: 1) To spoil or ruin something. "We can't let the rival *swashbucklers* get the *treasure*—we have to somehow *spoliate* their plans." 2) The fact of spoilage or ruination. "Take it from me, when ye put *butter broth* and hot sunshine together fer prolonged periods of time, *spoliation* will occur." 3) A person who spoils or ruins things.

"We drew the short straw in the pirate draft pick this year."

"*Futtocks!* Who's left?"

"*Spoliator* Sam."

"Well, that's just splendid, that is."

spreads much cloth: When pirates and sailors of yore said, "She *spreads much cloth*," they were talking about a ship with a lot of sails. Nowadays, pirates of either sex may use this expression to describe someone thought to be carrying excellent cargo aloft or below in either the *fore* or *aft* ends.

"Buxom Betty *spreads much cloth*" or "*Jolly* Polly *spreads much cloth*," or, as *ribald wenches* might have opined:

"I bet *Cheese-Cutter* Charlie *spreads much cloth*."

"You know what they say—where there's a big *cheese cutter,* there's a big cheese."

spree: Most simply put, a *spree* is a lively outing. But its possible roots reflect a heritage more fitting to piracy, since the word may have descended from "spreath," a Scottish word for cattle stolen from someone else.

"How was yer raidin' *spree*?"

"'Twas *thunderin'* good. We came back with lots o' *booty.*"

spruce boot: If you're getting tired of all these creative names for pirates with *wooden legs*, suck it up. "Hey, *Spruce Boot,* lend us yer limb—we need to club this barkeep into submission."

square rigged: A way of rigging a ship's sails so that they sit at right angles to the long axis of the ship. Seen from above, a *square-rigged* ship would look like this: ‡

squire: A *squire* was a young nobleman who attended to a knight and was ranked just below a knight. In a more general sense, it can also mean either a local judge or simply a country gentleman, usually with substantial assets (for example, Squire Trelawney in *Treasure Island*). Pirates may also use it derisively. In the same way that modern speakers might refer to a butterfingered mate as "Captain Klutz," sharp-tongued *buccaneers* might say, "There goes *Squire Fumble Fist* again."

stabber: Any kind of sword or knife (for obvious reasons). Take, for instance, this wholly fictional pirate advertisement:

Sale On All

Flats and Sharps

Bilboes, Bodkins, Cheese Toasters, Cutlasses, Iron Toothpicks, Smiters, etcetera.

Get eight pieces for eight *pieces of eight*

at

Crazy Beard's *Stabber* Emporium

This week only.

starboard: When you're standing on the deck of a ship facing forward, *starboard* is on your right.

stash it there: Stop it! Be quiet! This phrase is particularly useful when someone who is learning to speak pirate corners you and decides to practice on you.

"So I can see fer meself that the *sea devil's* just *spoliatin'* fer a conflict o' some kind, so I pulls out me *smiter,* but then me *galligaskins* fall down and me *plank shank* gets stuck in a lump of oozin' *oakum* and I fall flat on me *Sunday face*—"

"*Stash it there, matey.*"

stern: The rear part of a ship's hull, or as *landlubbers* say, "The back end of the boat." Can also be used to describe pirate posteriors. "Ripped Roger's got quite the tight little *stern* back there."

stiff rumped: Strictly speaking, this colorful expression means "proud," but today's pirates are more likely to use it in the sense of "tight-assed," describing someone who is prudish, conservative or simply no fun (which logically follows from prudish and conservative).

"The new cap'n's got a *right stiff rump*—he won't let us use captured admirals fer target practice anymore."

stomach worm gnaws: Hunger pangs. "The *stomach worm gnaws, mateys.* We'd best *choke the luff* and *git ourselves 'round* some *salmagundi*."

storm breeders: Heavy clouds. "Them *storm breeders* are weavin' a *proper devil's* tablecloth."

strumpet: A harlot. *Wench,* harlot, *strumpet* and *trollope* are all words that started out as ways to negatively describe women, suggesting sinfulness because of sexual intercourse unsanctioned by marriage. Observant readers may have noticed that in recent years, sexual intercourse unsanctioned by marriage has become a pleasure happily embraced and eagerly pursued by many people. In view of that, all of the words listed above have been rehabilitated as affectionate if enjoyably *naughty* ways of addressing women who you wish to suggest are *hugsome* (whether the woman in question wishes to be so-addressed is a separate issue, but one that has been with us for hundreds of years and is not going anywhere soon).

stump cups: Boots.

"Yer *fecket* and *sit upons* go real nice with yer *stump cups*."

"Fall out o' the fruit tree this mornin', *matey?*"

suck up some corn juice: To consume an alcoholic beverage. "Let's find ourselves a *gargle factory* and *suck up some corn juice.*"

Sunday face: Bum; buttocks. We can only assume that this saying came about because on Sundays, all a pirate does is sit around on a church pew listening to sermons and such-like. Never mind that pirates are among the least likely of churchgoers, the expression is simply too good not to use. "Does that *Sunday face* of yers git sore from settin' about all the time like a *belly-gutted shack rag?*"

suresby: A reliable person. "Dependable Dan's a *right suresby.*"

swab: A mop used for mopping the *deck;* to mop the *deck;* the person who mops the *deck;* an affectionate insult. In modern popular culture, *swab* is a nickname for any sailor, in the same way *salt* is used. Pirates can feel confident in using *swab* as a term to suggest that the person being described is completely average at what they do:

"Ye're callin' yerselves Plunder and Pillage Specialists? Git over it! Ye're a bunch o' *deck swabs!*"

swag: *Treasure;* loot; takings. Nowadays when movie stars go to gala events, they get *swag* bags, which are satchels of loot loaded with designer brands and the like. At a pirate gala, things might go like this:

"Look, our *swag* bags have i-*Parrots* in them."

"I hear they can store a whole lot o' sayin' and songs."

"Try gettin' 'em to shut up, though."

"And the cleanup is somefin' awful."

swashbuckler: A "buckler" was a small shield carried by swordsmen to ward off the blows of their opponents. To "swash" meant to make a loud noise (presumably by striking your opponent's buckler). Since Elizabethan times, *swashbuckler* has meant a swaggering showoff, possibly someone who swashes his own buckler to get the attention of others.

"How do ye like me *swashbucklin'*?"

"Oh, why don't ye go swash somebody else's buckler fer a change!"

swilker: To splash about. Overheard during a raiding expedition in which some novice pirates were attempting to quietly row ashore at night: "You call that rowin'? I've heard *spigot suckers swilker* less when *bleedin' the monkey!*"

swill: To drink greedily; any weak or inferior alcoholic beverage; *bilge*. "How can ye *swill* that *swill* when it tastes like *swill?*"

swish: Sea spray. "Step lively there, *Spruce Boot*. All that *swish* be makin' the *deck right clarty.*"

swive: To have sex with.

"I hear that Well-Endowed Willy *spreads much cloth*."

"Doesn't necessarily mean he's a good *swive,* though."

swivel: To spin or rotate back and forth. *Swivel* guns were small *deck* guns that could be mounted any-where on the *deck*, and any self-respecting pirate ship had more than a few. In general, though, *swivel* is a word that rolls off the tongue with a pleasingly pirati-cal flavor, and aspiring speakers of Pirate should use it as they see fit.

swizzle: Beer.

swoon: Ladies faint, *maidens swoon* and *wenches* are generally unfazed by whatever you throw at them. *Swooning* doesn't happen a whole lot in the pirate community, but it may very well happen *because* of the pirate community. "You see m'lord, m'lady thought she heard a band of pirates swarming over the *rails,* and she *swooned*. When you unexpectedly entered the cabin just now, I was resuscitating her with the kiss of life…Yes, m'lord, I know there aren't any pirates—Madam, would you please disengage yourself while I still have a head on my shoulders."

T

tail wagger: A dog. To judge from the expressions listed in this book, pirates were dog people as opposed to cat people. You only have to compare the affectionate put-downs that describe cats—*long-tailed beggars, purring bandits* and so on—to the jovial expressions to describe dogs—*magnificent furry beasts, panting chums* and *tail waggers.*

tapping the admiral: The desperation of a person who would drink anything. "Admiral" was a different way of saying "monkey" (as in *bleeding the monkey*) and so implies desperation in the search for drink.

"What'll ye have?"

"*Bombo, swill, bumclink*…what have ye."

"Really *tappin' the admiral,* ain't ye?"

teeth: Ships' cannons. "Let's show 'em our *teeth, matey.*" That is, "Let's begin firing on the enemy."

telltale shake: During the age of sail, sometimes one sailor would be required to hold on to the lower end of a rope, while a second sailor, aloft in the rigging, refastened or adjusted the top end. When the task was finished and the rope could be let go, the sailor up top would give it the *telltale shake*, a signal to his mate to loosen his grip. In pirating circles, though, this expression can also mean any secret, pre-arranged signal between two co-conspirators.

"When ye're ready to slip out fer a *nose warmer* just give me the *telltale shake*."

terrapin (swift as a): *Terrapins* are water turtles (often enjoyed as an ingredient in *salmagundi*). Like most turtles, they are not particularly speedy on land, and *swift as a terrapin* means someone who is not swift at all. "*Ahoy,* me *hearties,* let me introduce ye to our new *deck swab,* Sluggish Pete. He may be *swift as a terrapin*, but I guarantee ye our decks will be clean enough to *choke the luff* on."

thick as the mainmast / mizenmast: Dense; slow on the uptake. Masts on old ships were as big around as a stocky adult, sometimes bigger. This is the pirate equivalent of "thick as a post," "dumb as a stump," "sharp as a sack of wet mice" and so on. "He's as *thick as the mizenmast*, that one is. Nice *aft*-end, though."

throatsome: Tasty; delicious (of food or *hugsome* pirates).

"This *grog* is *thunderin' throatsome*."

"This batch o' *salmagundi* is *proper throatsome*."

"Handsome Ned looks a *right throatsome* sort of *rogue.*"

thundering: An emphatic adjective of many uses. 1) It can mean "very," as in "That's a *thunderin'* bright *grog blossom* ye're sportin', *matey.*" 2) It also serves as a general curse in much the same way as "damn." "How are we supposed to git any piratin' done with this *thunderin' hurleblast* goin' on?" 3) It can also emphasize anything large, fine or excellent.

"That be a *thunderin'* great new ship ye've captured, *matey.*"

"Well, ye know what they say, a vessel stolen is a vessel earned."

tipping the grampus: Dumping a sleeping pirate out of his hammock. "Arr, *mateys,* Snoozin' Charlie's livin' up to his name again. Let's *tip the grampus!*" (See also *grampus.*)

toady: A sycophant; a yes-man; an ass-kisser. "Hoy, *Squire Toady.* If ye can pry yer lips off the Cap'n's *double juggs* fer long enough, there's *bilge* cleanin' to be done."

toke: A drink made from honey in Madagascar. "Shall we *get ourselves around a toothful* of *toke?*"

tompion: A large wooden plug placed in the mouth of a cannon to keep its innards dry when it is not in use. Pirates are also fond of using it to mean "shut up" or "put a cork in it" (such as in *"Tompion* yer tongue, *matey."*)

tongue-bilge: Excessive or nonsensical talk. (See also *palaver.*)

toothful: A small measure of liquor. "Shall we have a *toothful* for our morning *livener?*"

tooth rot: Sugar. "Java, barkeep. Twice the *tooth rot* and double the *butter broth."* You will probably recognize this as a pirate ordering a coffee with two sugars and two creams.

tossing matches while the boat burns: Making an already bad situation worse. This expression is often used when female pirates are *skirting cannonballs.* "They were already wastin' all their time sword fightin' *hammer and tongs,* but then one of 'em pulls out his *hand cannon,* and they starts shootin' at each other. *Tossin' matches while the boat burned*, they was. So then me and my band of sexy *viragos* swooped in and took the ship with the *treasure* on it."

tough-knuckled: Describes an affectionate if abrasive compliment, especially toward anything that is basically good, but still has rough edges. For instance, a *tough-knuckled* compliment would be, "Ye're tough as a callous but I love ye anyway, me old *fungus!"*

travado: A heavy squall or sudden gust of wind.

"*Egads!* What a *travado* that was!"

"Nay, 'twas just Sneezey Mike greetin' this *proud mornin'.*"

treasure: Riches; money; loot. Some pirates say they enjoy the lifestyle, but let's face it, a lifestyle it ain't. They're in it for the *treasure*.

tremble: To quake or shudder. This is another word that comes trippingly off pirate tongues and can be used where appropriate. "The name *Bottom Wind* Bill sets decent folk (or at least folk with noses) a *tremblin'* in their boots."

trencher / trencher-wipe: *Trenchers* were wooden plates or platters for serving food. A *trencher-wipe* could be either the rag used for wiping *trenchers* off, or the person doing the wiping. From this, it can also mean any sort of wait staff or server. "*Ahoy! Trencher-wipe!* I've spilt me *bumclink*—give us a wipe."

trollope: A promiscuous woman of easy virtue, but sometimes used now as an affectionate form of address for someone's (presumably, female) bunk-mate. (See also *strumpet* and *wench*.)

trounce: To thoroughly defeat. "Of course we *trounced* the Royal Navy—they drink *grog*; we drink *rum*."

trout face: A person with a downcast countenance. *"Ahoy, trout face.* What's the matter? Did somebody skewer yer *parrot?"*

trunions: Nubs of metal on either side of a cannon for it to rest on and that allow it to tilt up and down. In pirate speak, it is sometimes (but seldom) used as slang for "feet," even though *trunions* on the side of a cannon are more like little stumpy arms. "Plant yer *Sunday face* and give yer *trunions* a rest."

U

unfurl: In a purely nautical sense, this refers to unrolling or unfolding a sail. But in pirate boudoirs, it can also mean to undress. "Ye're *unfurlin'* me with yer eye."

ungothroughsome: In Elizabethan England, there was a movement afoot to purge the English language of any words borrowed from Latin. The famous example is "impenetrable," which was to be replaced with *ungothroughsome*. The academics leading the charge lost the battle, and *ungothroughsome* is now just a quaint relic of a dead linguistic cause. However, it does *sound* incredibly piratical and is simply too delicious a word not to include. You can easily imagine a boatload of *scurvy* dogs deciding that "impenetrable" was too much of a *sleeveboard* and substituting *ungothroughsome* instead. "*By Gar,* these fortress walls are imperturbable…impenient…defenestrated—they're *ungothroughsome* is what they are!"

unrove his lifeline: Departed this life. "Rove" means to twist and stretch fibers ready to be spun into thread, so in this sense, *unrove* means essentially the same thing as unravel, and the image of someone's lifeline unraveling is clear enough.

"What's the matter with Gullible Gus today?"

"Some shady *parrot* monger sold him a bird whose *lifeline was unrove.*"

"And he bought it anyway?"

"Well, 'twas nailed to the perch and apparently presented quite a life-like appearance."

uppish: Proud; arrogant; stuck-up. "That's *Uppish* Roland—he's got a solid gold, jewel-encrusted eye patch, and he ain't even missin' an eye."

V

veer: To suddenly change direction. It usually describes a ship or vessel that *veers* off course, but it can also describe someone walking erratically or unsteadily.

"There goes *Grog Blossom* Bob again—*three sheets aft* and *veerin'* from table to table lookin' fer half-full glasses."

"At least he looks fer glasses that are half-full and not half-empty."

"Arr, he may be a *spigot sucker* but at least he's an optimist."

venture: Any effort or excursion made in the hopes of turning a profit or achieving some spectacular success. For pirates, any worthwhile venture almost certainly involves the acquisition of large amounts of *treasure* without paying for it.

"Let's raise a *noggin* to the success of our *swag*-stealin' *venture*."

veritable: 1) A word that intensifies things. "Yer *bottom wind* be a *veritable hurleblast*." 2) Virtually;

nearly; in all but name. "Yer *bottom wind* be a *veritable hurleblast.*"

victuals: Hearty, tasty food. "Shall we *away* to a *grub dive* in quest of some *throatsome victuals?*"

virago: A large, strong or intrepid woman; in short, just the sort likely to become a pirate and to attract other pirates. "That's *Virago* Viv. When she's finished havin' her way with ye, she *heaves* ye bodily *overboard* and calls, 'Next!'"

vowel mauler: An indistinct speaker. To judge from their numerous difficulties with *sleeveboards,* many a pirate must have been a *vowel mauler.*

"*Daggerknee* to the reef we found a *dillywreck* packed with *sparrow grass.*"

"What did he just say?"

"I have no idea."

W

weatherly: A well-trimmed ship; anything orderly or well kept.

"Statuesque Steve cuts a *right weatherly* figure."

"Too bad he's *bent on a splice* with Pulchritudinous Polly."

weevil: Any one of a number of beetles that likes to eat plants and things made from plants. A *weevil* infestation on board a ship is a bad thing, but notwithstanding, kind-hearted pirates may use the word as an affectionate form of address to children. "Care fer a skull-and-*crossbones*-shaped lollipop, ye little *weevil?*"

wench: 1) A girl or young woman, especially a peasant. 2) A wanton or promiscuous woman. Pirates use *wench* as a humorous and affectionate form of address with most women they encounter, especially when ordering tankards of ale or *mutchkins* of *rum. Wenches* are usually highly desirable because of their comely looks, lively personalities and the inner strength that comes from mastering the ever-present urge to bring a heavy metal pitcher down on the head of pirates who call them *wenches.* Unfortunately, some pirates interpret a flagon to the head as a sign of affection or encouragement.

Which way does the wind lie?: Another way of saying, "What is the matter?" Make sure you've had a shower before using this expression, or an unpleasant surprise may await.

"Yer countenance be all contorted-like. *Which way does the wind lie?*"

"Well, on the wrong side o' you, *matey,* that's fer sure. *By Gar* there's an atmosphere of *bilge* about ye that's makin' me *cheese cutter* curdle."

whittle: To carve by chipping out small pieces. "If ye don't stop tappin' yer *plank shank,* I'll practice *whittlin'* on yer face."

with a will: Zeal and energy. "Dig *with a will,* me *hearties!* £900,000 lies below."

within an ace of ruin: Frighteningly close to disaster. "If we run out o' gunpowder, we'll be *within an ace of ruin.*"

wobble shop: A pub, so-called because of the wobbly effect that the *libations* consumed therein are prone to produce. "Let's put away more than a few *mutchkins* of *anti-abstinence* at the nearest *wobble shop.*"

wooden leg: Something all pirates should have, even if they don't need one. The leg itself or its wearer can also be called *plank shank, lumber limb, pine foot, spruce boot* and so on.

woolding: A particularly nasty form of pirate torture in which a loop of rope is tightened around the victim's head until his or her eyeballs pop out.

"*Egads,* man. Ye look as though ye've just been *woolded!*"

"Arr, I just saw Ugly Joe without his hat on! *By Gar* it nearly killed me!"

worm eaten: Literally eaten by worms, but figuratively anything mangy, worn out or generally past its prime.

"*Hearties,* this is *Scurvy* Scott, yer new quartermaster."

"Looks a bit *worm eaten,* don't he?"

X–Z

X: The letter that marks the spot.

zephyr: A light, passing breeze.

"Me *paramour* has breath like a pleasant *zephyr.*"

"More than I can say fer you, *matey.*"

Afterword

Celebrating Your Pirate Heritage

If any further proof of the excellentness of Lingua Pira is needed, consider this: in recent years, wenches, rogues and swashbucklers from all around the world have vocally celebrated September 19 as "International Talk Like a Pirate Day." On this day, a global chorus of "Arrs," "Ahoys" and "Avasts" can be heard to issue forth from all corners of the earth.

Why do people do this? Because by momentarily speaking like a pirate, we *become* pirates. If you haven't already, try it. Just stand up and say aloud, "Shiver me timbers!" Not only will you feel a rush of roguish optimism, but for a brief instant, the seven seas will become your own personal playground: your trunk overfloweth with gold, your parrot screecheth "pieces of eight," and all is well with the world.

Lingua Pira means that *every* day can be Talk Like a Pirate Day. Don't forget that you have just as much right to be a pirate as anyone else does; after all, some are born pirates; some achieve piratehood; and others have piracy thrust upon them. (Hint: You should always aim to be the one doing the thrusting, meaning that you are the pirate in the picture.)

Whether you're looking to expand your circle of friends (in which case you may want to take up a hobby that has a bigger market share than talking like a pirate), meet that someone special (which, if you're a woman, shouldn't be difficult since there's probably no easier place to meet single men than at a pirate festival) or just want to reconnect with the heritage of your ancestors (yes, yes, we'd ALL like to think we're descended from pirates—got any proof?), Lingua Pira can help you to do all of these things. But mainly, what you should aim to get out of speaking Lingua Pira is a sense of fun.

Fare thee well, smooth sailing, and may much treasure be yours.

Notes on Sources

"Serious" linguists who may be considering using this book as a source should do anything but. Most of the terms and expression herein *are* genuine slang terms taken from the sources that follow and, as often as not, date from the period 1680–1730 (the Golden Age of Piracy) or earlier. However, I have also taken considerable liberties with the secondary meanings of words. For instance, *bottom wind* really is a nautical expression to describe waves that appear on the water's surface, seemingly for no reason. But the choice to make it a synonym for "farting" was mine and mine alone.

Similar instances occur throughout the book, but a few of the more prominent ones are *bouncer, channel groper, spreads much cloth, dabberlack, dead cargo, damsel, futtocks, fecket, firkin, frigate, fucus maximus, long-necked goose, moss bonker, Neptune's goblets, ramrod* and *weatherly*. Again, these are just a few examples—people whose burning love of language requires them to know which terms are genuine can consult the works listed.

There are also a few expressions that as far as I know, I have completely made up by combining already existing slang phrases into new ones. These include the expression "Lingua Pira" itself, as well as *barmy in the crumpet, between-the-sheets chum, butter broth, chicken jems/jewels, el canino, English gratitude, French courtesy, grub dive, haberdasher of grabbery, heaving the grog, hurling yer hard tack, Irish tea, listing groundward, lumber limb, magnificent furry beast, panting chum, pine foot, plank shank, purring bandit, Scottish beef, seven pieces short of eight* (my personal favorite), *skirting the cannonballs, spewing the oakum, splinter toe, spruce boot, stump cup, tail wagger, throatsome, tossing matches while the ship burns* and *tooth rot.* The rest of the expressions in the Lexicon were found in the various works listed, though again, in some cases I have enhanced their definitions.

And finally, once again I remind readers that this book is called *How to Speak Pirate,* and not *How Pirates Really Spoke.*

Browning, D.C. (Ed.). *Roget's Thesaurus: The Everyman Edition*. London, England: Octopus Books, 1982.

Farmer, J.S. & W.E. Henley. *Slang and Its Analogues*. New York, NY: Arno Publishing (A Publishing and Library Service of the New York Times), 1970.

Hendrickson, Robert. *The Facts on File Encyclopedia of Word and Phrase Origins*. New York, NY: Checkmark Books, 2000.

Morris, William (Ed.). *The Heritage Illustrated Dictionary of the English Language*. Boston, MA: Houghton Mifflin Company, 1979.

Partridge, Eric & Jacqueline Simpson. *The Penguin Dictionary of Historical Slang*. Middelsex, England: Penguin Books Ltd., 1972.

Smyth, W.H. *The Sailor's Lexicon*. New York, NY: Hearst Books, 2005.

Telfer, Geordie. *Real Canadian Pirates: Buccaneers & Rogues of the North*. Edmonton, AB: Folklore Publishing, 2007.

Geordie Telfer

Geordie Telfer is a writer, actor and artist. As a child, he practiced flying by leaping onto a beanbag chair, and his dream job was to become Batman. Unfortunately, neither ambition turned out, but his passion for adventure remains.

Geordie has been an assistant director, a freelance set carpenter and a web and television writer. He worked extensively on deafplanet.com, the first TV show and website in American Sign Language, and has written several nature documentaries. Geordie has always been interested in the swashbuckling adventurers we call pirates and has written another non-fiction book on the subject.